Luan Ferr

Cosmic Spirituality
Connecting with Beings of Light for the Awakening of the Soul

Copyright
Original Title: Espiritualidade Cósmica
Copyright © 2023, published in 2024 by Luiz Antonio dos Santos ME.

This book explores spiritual practices, meditation and connection with cosmic energies, providing a guide to self-knowledge and the expansion of consciousness. It is intended to inspire personal and spiritual development, but is not a substitute for medical, psychological or therapeutic guidance.

Cosmic Spirituality
Second Edition

Second Edition Production Team
Author: Luan Ferr
Proofreading: Virginia Moreira dos Santos
Graphic Design and Layout: Arthur Mendes da Costa
Cover: Anderson Casagrande Neto
Translation: Emily Clarke

Publication and Identification
Cosmic Spirituality / By Luan Ferr
Ahzuria Publishing, 2024
Categories: Body, Mind and Spirit / Spirituality
DDC: 158.1 - CDU: 613.8
Copyright Notice
All rights reserved to:
Booklas Publishing/ Luiz Antonio dos Santos ME
This book may not be reproduced, distributed or transmitted, in whole or in part, by any means, electronic or printed, without the express consent of the copyright holder.

Summary

- Foreword 5
- 1 Cosmic Spirituality 9
- 2 Teachings and Cosmic Philosophy 12
- 3 Meditation Practices 15
- 4 Communication with Beings of Light 21
- 5 Applications of Cosmic Spirituality 27
- 6 Self-discovery and Self-knowledge 33
- 7 Emotional Transformation and Inner Healing 40
- 8 Intuition and Psychic Abilities 43
- 9 Expanding Individual Consciousness 52
- 10 Virtues and Values of the Beings of Light 56
- 11 The Transformative Power of the Cube of Light ... 59
- 12 Fundamentals of Cosmic Meditation 63
- 13 Meditation for Connection with the Source 66
- 14 Deepening the Connection 69
- 15 Cosmic Starship Meditation 72
- 16 Integrating Meditation into Everyday Life 75
- 17 The Higher Self 80
- 18 Communication Techniques 84
- 19 Channeling and Messages 87
- 20 Spiritual Guidance and Personal Growth 91
- 21 Co-creation with the Higher Self 104
- 22 Energetic Principles 108
- 23 Energy Alignment Exercises 117
- 24 Healing and Balance 123

25 Energy Centers 139
26 Energetic Alignment and Lifestyle 145
27 Conscious Manifestation 159
28 Creative Visualization 163
29 Empowering Manifestation 168
30 Aligned Co-creation 175
31 Levels of Consciousness 180
32 Expansion of Consciousness 183
33 Higher Dimensions and Beings of Light 188
34 Spiritual DNA 192
35 Integrating the Expansion of Consciousness 196
36 Harmony of Nature with the Universe 201
37 Relationships Deep Connections 204
38 Service to Others 208
Acknowledgements 211

Foreword

Spirituality is an intrinsic characteristic of the human condition. From birth, every being unconsciously feels an emptiness that can only be filled by something greater than themselves. This search for the transcendent is universal, but the diversity of experiences, cultures and thoughts makes it difficult to identify a single path as "the right one". With so many forms of faith and spirituality available, the challenge is to find the one that resonates with the essence of each individual.

The human being, in essence, is the result of a multitude of variants, which makes them unique in their perceptions and understandings. What may seem natural and obvious to one person may sound incomprehensible or even absurd to another. Just as it is not possible for a single perspective to cover all ways of thinking and feeling, it is also unreasonable to assume that there is a single form of spirituality capable of meeting the diversity of human consciousness.

After extensive studies, consultations with masters from different traditions and confrontations of ideas based on research and experience, an essential conclusion has emerged: all the forms of spirituality we know represent only a small fraction of the vastness of Universal Consciousness. These forms are manifestations that the greater consciousness, or Divine Source, has found to establish a connection with human beings, adapting to the limits of each person's understanding. Dividing itself into countless facets, this consciousness molds itself to human particularities, offering paths that guide us on our journey of self-discovery.

Within this vast spiritual field, the Beings of Light play a fundamental role. These highly evolved beings inhabit higher dimensions and offer humanity guidance and support on its spiritual journey. From the earliest times, when humanity's ancestors still inhabited caves, the Beings of Light were already present, helping the development of human consciousness. Cave paintings, such as those in the Chauvet Cave in France, which date back 36,000 years, suggest a deep spiritual connection that already existed at that time.

Throughout history, the Beings of Light have been recognized in different ways, depending on each culture's ability to interpret them. From angels to gods, their manifestations have varied, but their essence has remained the same: they are cosmic guides who help humanity understand its connection with the Divine Source and universal interconnectedness. Today, scholars and practitioners prefer to call them simply

Beings of Light, recognizing in them a universal expression of love, compassion and wisdom.

These beings not only observe, but actively assist in the spiritual evolution of humanity. Through channelings, personal experiences and transcendental encounters, many people report feeling their presence, which brings peace, guidance and healing. Their wisdom transcends the limits of time and space, offering teachings that connect human beings to the vast energy network of the cosmos.

Cosmic Spirituality is an approach that unites the various forms of faith in an integrated model, based on principles such as unconditional love, compassion and interconnectedness. Recognizing that all beings are connected by a universal energy web is the first step towards understanding the dimension of cosmic consciousness and the role of the Beings of Light.

In this context, practices such as meditation, introspection and self-development are indispensable tools for expanding consciousness. Meditation, for example, not only calms the mind, but opens portals to higher dimensions, allowing you to experience states of peace and clarity. These practices help to nurture the divine spark that resides within you, connecting you with the infinite flow of cosmic energy.

Another fundamental aspect is the search for balance and harmony. Cosmic Spirituality emphasizes the importance of aligning body, mind and spirit, promoting a balanced life that honors both material and spiritual needs. This holistic approach also includes valuing nature as an essential part of this universal connection.

Spiritual transformation is inseparable from inner healing. Energy healing techniques, such as those taught by the Beings of Light, help to release negative patterns and awaken the innate healing power that exists within each of us. By embracing transformation, you free yourself from limitations and expand your potential, allowing your consciousness to flourish at higher levels.

This book is an invitation for you to embark on a journey of expanding your consciousness and connecting with the ancient wisdom of the Beings of Light. By exploring the teachings and practices presented here, you will have the opportunity to discover new dimensions of yourself and the universe. Open your mind and heart to this experience, allowing the words and teachings of the Beings of Light to guide you towards a deeper understanding of life and the vastness of cosmic consciousness.

May this journey inspire the awakening of your true essence and reveal the infinite beauty of your connection with the cosmos.

1
Cosmic Spirituality

The Beings of Light are fascinating cosmic entities that arouse the curiosity and admiration of those who seek to explore spirituality. This book delves into the origins and unique characteristics of these beings, explaining who they are and what their role is in spirituality in general.

The Beings of Light are a highly evolved civilization whose wisdom and knowledge transcend the boundaries of space and time. They are believed to have reached such an advanced stage of consciousness that they are able to access higher dimensions, connecting with cosmic wisdom and the Source of all that exists. Their inter-dimensional access allows them to dive into lower dimensions to assist in the spiritual evolution of beings of lesser light, such as humans.

One of the most striking characteristics of the Beings of Light is their deep connection with the energy of Light. They are known for their high energetic vibration and ability to radiate unconditional love. This radiation is considered healing and transformative, capable of awakening consciousness and promoting physical, emotional and spiritual healing.

They are extremely compassionate and altruistic beings. Their essence is permeated by a deep sense of service to others and universal love. They believe in the importance of contributing to collective well-being, as well as in each person's ability to manifest their maximum potential within the limitations that the human condition allows.

The Beings of Light are also known for their wisdom and knowledge. They have a deep understanding of universal principles and the laws that govern the cosmos. Through meditation and connecting with cosmic wisdom, you will be able to receive insights and revelations that will help you in your spiritual awakening and individual growth.

Another interesting characteristic of the Beings of Light is their ability to communicate telepathically. They are proficient at transmitting and receiving information through the mind, without the need for words or verbal language. This form of subtle communication allows for the exchange of direct knowledge and teachings, facilitating the transmission of messages, wisdom and spiritual guidance.

In Cosmic Spirituality, the connection with Beings of Light is often sought for healing, guidance and expansion of consciousness. They can manipulate healing energy to work towards restoring energy balance and activating spiritual DNA.

Knowing the origin and characteristics of the Beings of Light is only the first step on the journey of exploring spirituality. Throughout this book we will delve deeply into their teachings, meditation practices, communication, application in everyday life, self-discovery, emotional transformation, development of intuition, expansion of individual consciousness, among other topics.

Get ready to be enchanted by the wisdom of the Beings of Light, allowing their presence to illuminate your spiritual path, opening up new horizons of growth and awakening.

2
Teachings and Cosmic Philosophy

Welcome to the wisdom of the Beings of Light, a philosophy based on a profound understanding of universal laws and the multidimensional nature of existence. You will be led into the depths of the teachings, and in doing so, open doors to a transformative journey of self-discovery and spiritual growth.

The Beings of Light recognize the interconnected nature of all things and understand that each of us is an active co-creator of our own reality. This philosophy is shared by many other spiritual traditions, and invites us to see beyond the limits of the human mind. It is an invitation to raise consciousness and expand understanding beyond everyday veils.

On your spiritual journey, the Beings of Light guide you to look within. They teach you that true power resides within and that the key to happiness and fulfillment lies in recognizing and cultivating your divine essence. Throughout this process, you are invited to explore limiting thought patterns, emotions and beliefs, releasing what no longer serves you and making room for the full expression of who you are.

The practice of self-transformation is one of the fundamental aspects of the teachings of the Beings of Light. In this inner dive, you find fertile ground for cultivating qualities such as love, compassion, gratitude and forgiveness. These virtues are fundamental to nourishing and strengthening your spiritual being, guiding you towards expanded consciousness.

Taking personal responsibility is one of the pillars of Cosmic philosophy. You are the creator of your reality and your choices have a significant impact on the whole. Through self-mastery, you become able to choose wisely the experiences you have, raising the vibrational standard of your being and everything around you.

Connecting with the Source (the divine energy that creates everything and which some call God) is the central aspect of the Cosmic journey. The Beings of Light invite you to reconnect with this energy through meditative practices and moments of contemplation explained throughout the book. By opening yourself up to receive guidance and inspiration from the source, you establish a deep bond with it that serves as a guide throughout your spiritual journey.

Cultivating awareness of the present moment is another valuable teaching from the Beings of Light. They invite you to slow down and be fully present in your daily experiences. It is in this magical and unique moment that you find true inner peace and the fullness of existence.

As you delve deeper into the teachings and the Cosmic philosophy, it becomes an inexhaustible source of inspiration and guidance, an invitation to expand consciousness, cultivate inner wisdom and live in harmony with universal principles. As you continue on this journey, you will discover that the wisdom of the Beings of Light is a blessing that will accompany you throughout your life, opening up paths of light and spiritual awakening.

3
Meditation Practices

Meditation plays a fundamental role in Cosmic Spirituality, allowing access to higher dimensions, reconnecting you with cosmic wisdom so that you experience a profound inner transformation.

One of the meditation practices widely used in Cosmic Spirituality is the Source connection meditation. This practice involves retreating into a quiet, silent space where you can direct your attention inwards, connecting with the divine energy that permeates the universe. As you open yourself up to receive this loving and transformative energy, you feel a deep sense of peace, clarity and connection with your highest self.

For didactic purposes, I present one of the ways of performing meditation that can be practiced by beginners.

Find a quiet place where you can sit comfortably. It can be on a chair or on the floor, the important thing is to find a position where you feel relaxed.

Close your eyes gently and start to focus your attention on your breathing. Observe the natural flow of the breath, without trying to alter it. Concentrate on the sensation of the air entering and leaving your body.

As you become more aware of your breathing, allow thoughts to gently dissolve. When they arise, don't worry, just let them pass without getting attached to them. Turn your attention to your breathing whenever you get distracted.

When you feel calmer, imagine yourself surrounded by a bright, loving light. Visualize this light as the energy of the Source, this divine energy is available to you. Feel the loving energy permeating your whole being.

Open yourself to receive this loving and transforming energy. Allow yourself to feel a deep sense of peace, clarity and connection with your highest self. Stay in this state of openness and receptivity for as long as you wish.

When you are ready to end the meditation, gradually bring your attention back to your physical body and the surrounding environment. Gently open your eyes. Take a few moments to reorient yourself before continuing with your daily activities.

Another meditation practice in Cosmic Spirituality is the spiritual DNA activation meditation. In this meditation, you should focus on visualizing your DNA structure bathed in a healing and purifying Cosmic light. This light acts as an activator, awakening the dormant potential within you, allowing you to access higher levels of consciousness.

In Cosmic Spirituality, meditation is also used as a tool for healing and balance. You can direct your attention to areas of the body that need healing, visualizing them being filled with Cosmic light and love. This practice releases energy blockages, promotes physical and emotional healing, restoring balance on all levels of being.

The Beings of Light teach the meditation of connection. In this practice, you open your heart and mind to receive guidance and insights from both the Beings of Light and other higher entities. You can direct your thoughts and intentions to establish telepathic communication with these beings, allowing their messages of wisdom and love to reach you.

For didactic purposes, here is a description of how you should do the connection meditation with the Beings of Light.

Find a quiet space where you can sit comfortably and concentrate. Make sure you are not interrupted during the meditation.

Close your eyes gently and start breathing deeply, allowing your body to relax with each exhale. Focus on relaxing your muscles and releasing any tension you may be feeling.

Bring your attention to your heart. Visualize it opening up like a blossoming flower, radiating light and love. Feel the sensation of warmth and expansion in your chest as you connect with the loving energy within you.

Mentally set the intention to connect with Beings of Light, including other higher entities. Feel open and receptive to their presence and guidance.

As your mind calms down, focus on sending thoughts and intentions to these beings. Visualize a telepathic connection forming, like a clear, bright line of communication between you and the Beings of Light.

Now allow the messages, guidance and insights to flow to you. Be open to receiving any images, words, feelings or intuitive knowledge that may arise. Trust your intuition and the wisdom of the Beings of Light.

Remain in this state of connection and reception for as long as you wish, absorbing the energies and information being transmitted.

When you are ready to end the meditation, thank the Beings of Light for their presence and guidance. Slowly bring your attention back to your physical body and the environment around you. Gently open your eyes and take a moment to refocus before returning to your daily activities.

In Cosmic Spirituality, meditation is also an opportunity to develop intuition and psychic abilities. By tuning in to your divine essence, you access information and insights beyond the limits of the rational mind. You can practice intuition expansion meditation, opening yourself up to intuitive insights and guidance that help you on your spiritual journey and in your daily choices.

An important practice in Cosmic meditation is the incorporation of the values and virtues of the Beings of Light. Take some time during your meditation to reflect on qualities such as love, compassion, gratitude, harmony and peace, as well as how to incorporate them into your life. This practice aligns your energy with Cosmic energy, helping you to live in harmony with high spiritual principles.

Meditation on Cosmic Spirituality is a journey of self-discovery, healing and expansion of consciousness. As you delve deeper into these meditative practices, you open up to a universe of possibilities and transformations. Meditation allows you to access the wisdom of the Beings of Light, integrating the Cosmic light into your daily life, awakening you to your true divine nature.

It's important to note that throughout the book you'll find complementary information that will help you understand these themes, for now the teaching is being dosed, like a medicine. This method ensures that by the end of the book your understanding of meditation techniques and their applications will be complete.

4
Communication with Beings of Light

In Cosmic Spirituality, communication with the Beings of Light plays an important role in the search for cosmic wisdom and guidance. The Beings of Light are highly evolved beings who offer knowledge and assistance to those who are open to receiving their messages. Learn about the different ways of communicating with the Beings of Light and the different ways of connecting with them.

One of the most common ways of communicating with the Beings of Light is through telepathy. The Beings of Light have an extraordinary ability to communicate directly through thought. They can transmit messages, insights and guidance directly into your mind, without the need for words. To establish this telepathic communication, it is important to open your mind and heart, be receptive and cultivate a state of calm and inner peace.

Although telepathy is not a natural human ability, you can train your mind to receive insights, to gradually open up this field of communication.

Here is an exercise that helps you develop telepathic communication skills to open yourself up to insights and messages from the Beings of Light.

Find a quiet, comfortable place where you can sit quietly. Make sure you are not interrupted during the exercise.

Close your eyes and gently begin to relax your body and mind through deep breaths. Inhale deeply through your nose, holding your breath briefly, and then exhale through your nose, releasing any tension or worry.

Focus on relaxing your mind, letting go of everyday thoughts and worries. Imagine a soft, calming light enveloping your mind, bringing clarity and serenity.

Visualize a connection forming between your mind and the minds of the Beings of Light. See a bright, clear line of communication establishing itself, connecting your mind to theirs.

While holding this visualization, mentally affirm your intention to open yourself to receive insights, messages and guidance. Be open and receptive to receiving this information with love and gratitude.

Begin to quieten your mind to enter a state of receptivity. Allow thoughts and images to arise, without judging or trying to control them. Be open to receiving any form of telepathic communication.

Maintain an attitude of patience, persistence and trust in the process. Remember that developing telepathic communication is a gradual process, so be kind to yourself and be willing to practice regularly.

After a few minutes of silence and receptivity, thank the Beings of Light for the connection and for the information that may have been transmitted. Express gratitude for their presence and guidance.

Slowly bring your attention back to your surroundings. Gently open your eyes and take a moment to reorient yourself before continuing your daily activities.

Remember that developing telepathic communication takes practice and perseverance. At first you'll only notice loose phrases and words, but as you continue to work on this skill, you'll notice a greater sensitivity in the insights and guidance that emerge in your mind.

Another way of communicating with the Beings of Light is through dreams and visions. During sleep, or in deep meditative states, you receive symbolic messages, images or experiences that connect you with Cosmic energy. These messages contain insights, guidance for your spiritual journey or answers to specific questions you are seeking. It is important to remember to record and interpret these dreams and visions, as they can contain valuable teachings.

Beings of Light can also communicate through sensations and intuitive perceptions. You may feel a loving and peaceful presence around you, or experience a sense of warmth and comfort in times of need. These sensations are signs that the Beings of Light are enveloping you with their energy, transmitting messages of support and encouragement. It's important to trust your intuition and be open to subtle perceptions.

Automatic writing is another technique you can use to communicate with the Beings of Light. In this practice, you allow your hands to move freely over the paper, writing intuitive messages without the conscious control of the mind. This technique allows the wisdom and teachings of the Beings of Light to flow through you, offering profound insights and revelations.

But for teaching purposes, here is a method that helps you develop the practice of automatic writing, allowing you to communicate with the Beings of Light.

Choose a quiet time and place where you can concentrate on practicing automatic writing. Make sure you have pen and paper available.

Sit comfortably, relax your body and mind with a few deep breaths. Let go of any day-to-day distractions or worries.

Focus on establishing a connection with the Beings of Light. You can do this by visualizing or affirming your intention to communicate with them through automatic writing. Ask for guidance and wisdom during the process.

Pick up the pen and start writing on the paper without consciously thinking about the words or their meaning. Let your hands move freely, following the intuitive flow. Don't worry about handwriting, spelling or grammar. The intention is to allow the information to flow spontaneously and intuitively.

Keep your mind relaxed and receptive. Be open to receiving messages, insights and revelations from the Beings of Light. Don't try to control or direct the process. Trust the wisdom and guidance transmitted.

As you write, pay attention to any feelings, images or intuitions that may arise in your consciousness. These may be additional information or clues about the communication you have received.

Keep writing until you feel that the communication has come to an end. This could be an intuitive sign or simply a feeling of completeness. Thank the Beings of Light for their communication and guidance.

When you have finished, take a moment to read and reflect on what you have written. These messages may contain profound insights and revelations about you, your spiritual journey or teachings.

Remember that automatic writing takes practice and patience. Not all automatic writing sessions may result in clear and meaningful messages. However, as you continue to practice and deepen your connection with the Beings of Light, the quality and clarity of the messages will improve.

When opening up to communication with the Beings of Light, it is essential to cultivate a state of trust, humility and gratitude. It is important to remember that this communication is a gift and an opportunity for your spiritual growth. As you connect more deeply with the Beings of Light, you will feel their loving presence more strongly and receive transcendental wisdom, which helps your spiritual evolution and the expansion of your consciousness.

5
Applications of Cosmic Spirituality

Cosmic Spirituality is not only a journey of discovery and inner growth, it can also be applied in practical and meaningful ways in your daily life.

One of the most important applications of Cosmic Spirituality is the practice of gratitude. The Beings of Light teach us to appreciate and value every aspect of life, from the smallest things to the greatest blessings. By cultivating an attitude of gratitude, you open up a positive and abundant perspective, recognizing the beauty and generosity of the universe. You can express gratitude on a daily basis, whether through affirmations, journal entries or simply by pausing to recognize the blessings present in your life. Look around, you're alive, isn't that a great reason to give thanks?

Another application of Cosmic Spirituality is the practice of compassion and unconditional love. The Beings of Light radiate energy of pure love and encourage everyone to extend this love to themselves and others. You can practice compassion by recognizing your shared humanity, treating others with kindness, empathy and respect. This includes not only those close to you, but also strangers, animals or the planet itself. By living with compassion, you contribute to the creation of a more harmonious and loving world.

The search for daily balance is another important application of Cosmic Spirituality. The Beings of Light teach that it is important to balance all areas of physical, emotional, mental and spiritual life. You can seek balance through practices such as self-care, meditation (already explained on previous pages), regular physical exercise, seeking moments of tranquillity or pursuing a healthy lifestyle. By prioritizing balance, you become more resilient, strengthening your connection with your spiritual essence and living with more harmony and fullness.

Cosmic Spirituality also invites you to live authentically, expressing your inner truth. The Beings of Light remind us that everyone has unique gifts, talents and purposes. By exploring and honoring these qualities, you align with your true essence and contribute to the world in a meaningful way. This involves listening to intuition, following your heart and having the courage to be authentic in all areas of life. By living your truth, you inspire and positively impact everyone around you.

This model of spirituality also encourages living in the present. Instead of getting stuck in the past or worrying about the future, this approach invites you to be fully present in the present moment. Remember, the past cannot be changed while the future is always uncertain. The Beings of Light teach you to connect with the present moment by cultivating awareness and mindfulness. You can do this by practicing meditation, by consciously observing your thoughts and emotions, or by simply appreciating the small moments of joy and beauty that occur in your daily life.

Here's one way to practice mindfulness: by reflecting on the present.

Practicing mindfulness can transform the way we deal with challenging situations on a daily basis. A simple and effective example is to reflect on the present and observe your emotional reactions more carefully and clearly.

It's natural to feel irritated when you hear something you don't like. However, this instinctive reaction can be an opportunity to exercise your ability to analyze the situation in a rational and balanced way. Ask yourself: Is what was said really a valid reason for causing this emotional upset? Often, upon reflection, you will realize that irritation does not contribute to a solution or to your well-being.

By adopting this reflective stance, you gain the chance to assess the real impact of the situation and choose a more constructive response. This practice not only improves your ability to face challenges, but also reduces unnecessary emotional strain, promoting a more serene and productive state of mind.

In addition, it's important to remember that your mental state has a direct influence on your body. Intense emotions trigger the release of chemical compounds in the brain, which can impact your mood and physical well-being. For this reason, cultivating the habit of observing and moderating your emotional reactions not only improves your quality of life, but also favors your mental and physical health.

By practicing mindfulness regularly, you develop a powerful skill: the ability to choose how you respond to circumstances, rather than reacting automatically. This change can be the key to living in a more balanced, conscious and happy way.

Just as we can learn to moderate our reactions to challenges, it's equally powerful to bring to mind moments that sparked joy and gratitude. Think of a special moment when you had reason to smile - be it a meaningful encounter, a personal achievement, or a simple gesture of kindness that warmed your heart. When you relive that moment, your mind naturally enters a state of gratitude, and this shift in focus generates a wave of well-being that can transform your day.

Gratitude is more than a passing emotion; it's a way to raise your energy vibration and strengthen your connection with the present. When we consciously analyze what motivated that smile, we open up space to understand our emotions and thoughts on a deeper level. This process encourages us to appreciate life's little blessings, promoting a sense of fulfillment that transcends external circumstances.

This practice of seeking gratitude also brings us closer to a broader spiritual dimension, called Cosmic Spirituality. By living in harmony with this perspective, you come to realize that every emotion, thought and action has an impact on the universal whole. Gratitude, in this context, not only benefits your mental and physical state, but also strengthens your connection with the cosmic energy that permeates everything around us.

By including gratitude in your mindfulness practice, you turn small moments into portals for self-reflection and spiritual growth. This creates a bridge between the inner world and the vastness of the cosmos, helping to build a life of balance, harmony and purpose. Remember: gratitude is not just a feeling; it is a conscious choice that can guide your journey towards a more connected and enriching existence.

By applying Cosmic Spirituality to your daily life, you transform the way you live and experience a deep connection with the universe and your true self. Gratitude, compassion, balance, authenticity and conscious presence are just some of the ways you can incorporate Cosmic teachings into your life. As you continue your journey through the pages of this book, you will explore more themes related to Cosmic Spirituality and discover how to further expand your consciousness by living in alignment with the wisdom of the Beings of Light.

6
Self-discovery and Self-knowledge

On the journey of Cosmic Spirituality, self-discovery and self-knowledge play a fundamental role. By going inward, you explore the recesses of your soul and uncover the true essence of your being. So dive into the process of self-discovery and follow the path of self-knowledge through cosmic wisdom.

Self-discovery is an invitation to explore who you are beyond the superficial layers of your personality. It is an invitation to connect with your spiritual essence, your inner truth and your unique gifts. In Cosmic Spirituality, each individual possesses the divine spark within them, a direct connection to the universe and to the Source of all that exists. By connecting with this spark, you open the door to a profound journey of self-discovery.

The journey to self-discovery is a profound process that requires effective practices of introspection and self-reflection. Among these practices is "Divine

Perspective," a powerful approach that invites you to observe your own thoughts and actions from an elevated, impartial and detached point of view.

What is the Divine Perspective Method? This method consists of adopting an omniscient vision, symbolically putting yourself in the place of a higher consciousness. It allows you to analyze your behaviors and thoughts more clearly, as if you were observing someone else instead of yourself. The central idea is to overcome the human tendency to justify or minimize one's own shortcomings and limitations.

Why is omniscient vision necessary? Because when you observe yourself, you are faced with the fact that you know yourself intimately - your intentions, fears and justifications. Unlike an outside observer, you can't hide anything from yourself. This complete transparency makes it impossible to ignore what needs to be faced, demanding a level of honesty that is the key to transformation.

To facilitate this practice, imagine that you are God or a Divine and Omniscient consciousness. As this higher consciousness, you observe your own actions, but with a neutral gaze, free of emotional judgments or justifications. This change of perspective allows you to see more honestly aspects that we often ignore when we analyze our actions in a conventional way.

How to apply the Divine Perspective?

Impartial Visualization: Close your eyes and imagine that you are an omniscient entity, observing your life as if it were a movie. Visualize your actions and thoughts as if they were being carried out by someone else.

Remove the emotional charge that usually accompanies self-reflection. Imagine that you have no emotional ties to the decisions or behaviors you are evaluating.

Question your actions impartially. For example: "Do these choices really reflect the higher values I wish to follow?" or "How have these actions impacted the people around me?"

Identify both constructive behaviors and those that need adjustment. Use this analysis to draw up an action plan for continuous improvement.

Why is Divine Perspective effective? This method allows you to transcend your human limitations, such as indulgence and self-sabotage, which often distort the way we evaluate our actions. By imagining yourself as a divine consciousness, you become able to observe your life with clarity and objectivity, recognizing both mistakes and successes in a balanced way.

In addition, the idea of adopting an omniscient vision - in which nothing can be hidden from your own analysis - eliminates any self-deception. When you are both the observer and the one being analyzed, you create a unique space to understand your deepest motivations and align your actions with a greater purpose.

Regular practice of this method not only promotes a deeper understanding of yourself, but also strengthens your ability to make decisions in line with your highest values and goals. By adopting the Divine Perspective, you turn self-reflection into a practical tool for personal and spiritual growth.

Try incorporating this method into your reflection routine. It will allow you to see yourself in a clear, honest and compassionate way, bringing out a more authentic version that is aligned with your essence.

To apply the Divine Perspective Method, follow these steps.

Set aside some quiet time to connect with yourself. Find a space where you can feel comfortable and without distractions.

Close your eyes and breathe deeply, allowing your mind and body to calm down. Imagine yourself sitting in front of another person who represents you.

From this perspective, you are God or the divine presence, the higher consciousness and you have all the knowledge and understanding of everything the other person in front of you is, has done and thinks.

Observe the other person's thoughts, actions and reasons from an omniscient perspective. Analyze the choices, motivations and behavioral patterns, try to understand how they align with your true essence and purpose, see where each decision, right or wrong, has taken the person in front of you.

As you examine different aspects of this person's life, ask questions like:

"How does this action or thought reflect the connection with the divine spark within this person?"

"Is this in harmony with their inner truth?"

"What can this person learn or should they have learned from this experience?"

Allow yourself to receive insights and intuitive guidance while remaining open and receptive to the answers that arise. Remember that when you put yourself in the place of the divine being, you are open to every form of energy in the universe. An interesting aspect of this perspective is that you can identify where your current actions will take you.

At the end of this analysis, give thanks for the wisdom shared and for the opportunity to get to know yourself from a broad perspective.

Remember that the Divine Perspective Method is a powerful tool for self-discovery, but it's also important to balance it with love and self-compassion. As you deepen this practice, you will receive new insights into yourself. By placing yourself in front of yourself, as the omniscient and omnipotent being, you can bless yourself and capture from the divine spark within you all the love and understanding you need to understand your purpose and your connection to the universe.

As you explore the Divine Perspective Method and other teachings from the Beings of Light throughout this book, you will discover how to incorporate these practices into your daily life and how to expand your consciousness. Together, we will continue on this journey of self-discovery, learning and spiritual growth, in search of a deep connection with cosmic wisdom.

As you advance on the journey of self-discovery, you begin to reconnect with your unique gifts and talents. Each of us possesses innate abilities with a unique contribution to make to the universe. Cosmic Spirituality encourages you to explore and honor these gifts so that they can manifest in your life. This involves practicing creative activities, developing specific skills or simply being willing to share your gifts with others. By expressing your authentic gifts, you find deep meaning in life and contribute to collective evolution.

On the path to self-knowledge, it is also important to embrace and integrate all parts of yourself. This means accepting both your luminous qualities and your shadows, recognizing that they are all part of your journey of growth. The Beings of Light remind you that it is through accepting and integrating these parts that you achieve inner harmony and balance. The practice of self-love and self-compassion plays a fundamental role in this process, allowing you to love and accept yourself.

As you delve deeper into self-discovery and self-knowledge, you discover that the journey never ends. You are constantly evolving, growing and expanding your consciousness. Cosmic Spirituality reminds us that self-discovery is a continuous process, a dance between being and becoming. As you reconnect with your spiritual essence, you open the door to a vast potential for growth and transformation.

7
Emotional Transformation and Inner Healing

In Cosmic Spirituality, emotional transformation and inner healing are fundamental pillars for spiritual growth and the awakening of consciousness. Emotions, being intrinsic expressions of human experience, carry profound messages that help us understand our relationship with the universe and with ourselves. However, when these emotions are not properly recognized and processed, they become sources of suffering, limiting our potential for evolution.

The Beings of Light, in their wisdom, teach us the importance of welcoming our emotions with love and compassion, allowing us to feel them fully. Honoring the presence of emotions, even the most challenging ones, is the first step towards integrating them and transforming them into tools for growth and self-discovery. This practice helps us understand that each emotion brings with it a valuable lesson, an opportunity to expand our consciousness.

Emotional transformation begins with awareness. This means being present and attentive to what we feel, acknowledging the existence of our emotions without judgment. We need to explore their origins and messages, asking ourselves: "What is this emotion trying to tell me?". By accepting and examining our emotions openly, we connect with the wisdom they offer, allowing them to become catalysts for inner transformation.

Cosmic Spirituality offers various practices to assist in the process of emotional healing:

Meditation is a powerful tool that helps us observe our emotions without identifying with them. During meditation, you can visualize your emotions as waves in the ocean, which come and go, while remaining anchored in your spiritual essence. This practice promotes detachment from negative emotional patterns and opens up space for states of balance and inner peace.

The practice of forgiveness is essential for releasing emotions that bind us to the past, such as resentment, guilt and regret. Forgiveness, both for oneself and for others, does not mean justifying harmful actions, but rather freeing oneself from the emotional weight they carry. This allows love and compassion to flow freely, restoring inner harmony.

Cultivating gratitude is a way of transforming negative emotions into positive ones. When we focus on the blessings present in our lives, even in difficult times, we raise our energetic vibration and strengthen our connection with the cosmos.

Although the journey of emotional transformation is deeply personal, external support can be invaluable. Seeking help from therapists, spiritual counselors or support groups creates a safe space to explore emotions and share experiences. This exchange of energy promotes collective healing and strengthens the individual journey.

It's important to remember that inner healing is not a destination, but an ongoing process. Each layer of emotion worked through leads to new discoveries and opportunities for growth. As we move forward, we expand our awareness and align with our true potential.

Emotional transformation, aligned with the teachings of the Beings of Light, is a reminder that we are constantly evolving beings. By welcoming our emotions with love and integrating them into our spiritual journey, we become channels of light and harmony, radiating balance to the world around us.

8
Intuition and Psychic Abilities

In Cosmic Spirituality, the development of intuition and psychic abilities is an essential part of the spiritual path. You are involved in subtle energies and understanding them is part of your growth as a multidimensional being. You will learn the importance of cultivating these abilities and understand how they help you on your journey of growth and expansion.

But before going any further, it may be important to clarify the holistic meaning of the term "subtle", so that the content of the chapter can be fully understood.

Within the holistic conception, the term "subtle" is used to describe something that is delicate, soft and may not be readily perceptible by the physical senses. It is the quality that goes beyond the material level and refers to energies, vibrations and non-physical aspects of reality.

In the holistic approach, everything in the universe is interconnected and governed by a web of energies and information. These subtle energies are present in all aspects of life, from human emotions to the nature that surrounds us. However, we can't always perceive them with our ordinary physical senses.

For example, intuition is considered a form of subtle knowledge. It is that inner voice that guides and provides insights and understandings beyond what rational thoughts can achieve.

In the context of intuition and spiritual development, being attuned to the subtle means being aware of the nuances of life, paying attention to the signs, synchronicities and patterns that manifest around you. This involves a greater sensitivity to the subtle energies that permeate the environment and one's own consciousness.

Intuition is the innate ability to access information beyond rational and logical knowledge. It is the inner voice, the deep wisdom that guides and connects you to the essence of the universe. By developing your intuition, you open up a direct channel of communication with cosmic wisdom and the Beings of Light.

One of the ways to develop intuition is through the practice of meditation (already explained on previous pages). When you quieten your mind, you become receptive to the subtle messages that arise. Meditation creates an inner space conducive to listening to intuition and recognizing its wise guidance. As you practice meditation regularly, you become more sensitive to the signs and synchronicities that the universe sends.

Another way to develop intuition and connect with your spiritual essence is by trusting and practicing techniques that allow you to get in touch with your own soul. The soul is the spiritual essence, it is what lives beyond the physical plane, it is your connection with the source of creation of all that exists. By cultivating an intimate relationship with your spiritual essence, you learn to recognize and trust the information you receive intuitively. This process involves developing authenticity and the ability to follow your inner truth, even when it goes against society's opinion or external expectations.

To connect with your spiritual essence, here are some practices you can adopt:

Self-knowledge: Take time to reflect on your beliefs, values and life purpose. Ask yourself about your passions, talents and what brings you meaning. By getting to know yourself better, you'll be getting closer to your spiritual essence.

Conscious observation: Keep your mind in the present moment, observe your thoughts, emotions and physical sensations. Learn to recognize patterns and automatic responses that arise. This increased awareness will allow you to connect more deeply with your inner truth.

Practice gratitude: Cultivate a state of gratitude, directing your attention to the blessings and moments of joy present on your journey. Gratitude opens the heart and strengthens your connection with your spiritual essence.

Intuitive writing: Take time to write freely, without censorship or judgment. Allow the words to flow intuitively, expressing your thoughts, emotions and insights. This practice helps you access your inner wisdom and deepens your connection with your spiritual essence.

Connecting with nature: Get close to nature and appreciate its beauty and serenity. Walk through a forest or park, contemplate the sunset or simply breathe in the fresh air, imagine the power involved in every creation you perceive, after all, you are part of it. You are the only life form within nature that is aware of its greatness, knows who you are and what you are. Nature was created and exists to enable you to have life. It has a healing energy and can align you with your spiritual essence.

Remember that each person has a unique spiritual journey, and the path to connecting with the spiritual essence can vary. Experiment with different practices, find the ones that resonate best with you. Be patient with yourself, as the process of connecting with your spiritual essence is continuous and requires dedication and self-compassion.

As you continue to explore the teachings of the Beings of Light in this book, you will find more insights and practices to deepen the connection with your spiritual essence. The journey of self-discovery and connection with your inner truth is a valuable and transformative quest, and a path worth walking.

Another important technique is the practice of inner listening. This involves tuning in to your inner voice, to the wisdom that arises from within you. As you learn to silence your mind and listen attentively, you receive valuable guidance and insights from the subtle realms. This practice also helps you to discern between the voice of the ego and the intuitive voice, allowing you to make decisions in line with your true self.

In addition to intuition, Cosmic Spirituality also values the development of psychic abilities, such as clairvoyance, clairaudience and telepathy. These abilities allow you to access information beyond the five physical senses, making connections with subtle planes of existence. To strengthen and develop these abilities, it is essential to dedicate time to practicing and improving your energetic sensitivity.

This simple, practical exercise can help you strengthen your energetic sensitivity and broaden your connection with the flow of energy around you.

Find a quiet place where you won't be interrupted. Sit comfortably in a position that allows you to keep your spine erect. Close your eyes and take a few minutes to connect with your breathing.

Take a few deep breaths, inhaling through your nose and exhaling through your mouth. With each breath, allow your mind to calm down, releasing tensions and worries. Imagine that, as you breathe out, you are letting go of everything that doesn't serve you at the moment.

After reaching a state of relaxation, direct your attention to the space around you. Imagine that you are immersed in a field of subtle energy. Feel this energy enveloping your body, like a light breeze or a gentle warmth. Allow yourself to perceive nuances and patterns in this energy, without haste or effort.

Then focus your attention on your hands. Imagine them being enveloped in a soft, welcoming light, as if they were radiated by a divine energy. Visualize this light flowing through your hands, moving harmoniously.

Pay attention to the sensations that arise. You may feel warmth, tingling, vibration or even a slight pulsation. Don't worry if you don't feel anything immediately; just be open to the experience.

As you feel this energy, imagine it intensifying. Visualize it filling your hands and gradually expanding to your arms, body and your entire energy field. Allow this light to bring a sense of balance, harmony and well-being.

When you are ready to end the meditation, slowly bring your attention back to your breathing. Breathe deeply once again, feeling present and connected. Open your eyes slowly and allow yourself to integrate the experience into your day.

As you regularly practice this meditation, your subtle perception will become sharper, and you will begin to notice the energy flows around you more clearly. This exercise can also pave the way for the development of psychic abilities, such as enhanced intuition and energetic sensitivity.

Remember that developing these skills requires time, dedication and patience. As you go deeper into your spiritual journey, it is important to purify and raise your own energy through practices such as meditation. Visualizing a white light enveloping your body and searching for inner harmony contributes to this process. With time and consistent practice, you will become increasingly attuned to the subtle energies around you and will be able to explore the vast potential of your psychic abilities.

Developing intuition and psychic abilities requires a balance between opening up to the spiritual world and anchoring yourself in everyday reality. It's important to remember that you are a multidimensional being, capable of accessing different levels of consciousness. However, you are also here on Earth to live human experiences and contribute to the transformation of the world.

When developing your intuitive and psychic abilities, you should always remember to use them responsibly and lovingly. They are powerful tools that help you on your spiritual journey in search of the truth, but they must also be integrated in a balanced way into your daily life.

As you continue to explore Cosmic Spirituality, it is important to remember that the development of intuition and psychic abilities is an ongoing process. It requires practice, patience and dedication, but the benefits are immeasurable. By opening up to the subtle world and trusting your inner wisdom, you will discover a new level of connection with the universe and with your own divine essence.

"Know thyself."

This iconic phrase was inscribed on the Oracle of Delphi, a shrine in Ancient Greece famous for its enigmatic answers and spiritual advice. Believed to have been written by the Greek philosopher Socrates, who valued the importance of self-knowledge as a path to wisdom and personal growth, this shows that self-knowledge is a centuries-old practice. By connecting with your spiritual essence and delving deeper into your journey of self-discovery, you open doors to a deeper understanding of yourself and the world around you. The phrase "Know thyself" reminds us of the importance of exploring values, beliefs and identities in order to live with authenticity and meaning.

9
Expanding Individual Consciousness

The expansion of consciousness is a fascinating journey, an invitation to explore the depths of one's being, transcending the limits of one's reality. In Cosmic Spirituality, the expansion of consciousness is considered the fundamental step in spiritual evolution, as it allows access to higher levels of understanding and wisdom.

As you embark on this journey of expanding your consciousness, you are invited to question your limiting beliefs and expand your horizons. Sometimes you are used to seeing the world from a narrow perspective, based on your past experiences and social conditioning. However, Cosmic Spirituality is the invitation to go beyond these limitations, exploring new dimensions.

As there is a lot of talk about "limiting beliefs" holistically, it is appropriate to explain the meaning of the term so that you are fully aware of what a "limiting belief" is and how it affects your life.

Limiting beliefs are deeply rooted convictions in your mind that act as invisible barriers, restricting your actions, decisions and the way you perceive the world and yourself. These beliefs are often formed throughout life, based on past experiences, misinterpretations of events and social or cultural conditioning. For example, thoughts such as "I'm not good enough", "I don't deserve success" or "Things never change for me" are common examples of limiting beliefs that shape your reality in a negative way.

These beliefs affect life in a significant way because they act as mental filters that determine how you react to different situations. They can limit your potential, prevent you from achieving your goals or even distort your perceptions, causing you to see challenges where there are opportunities. Because they are unconscious most of the time, these beliefs operate in the background, influencing your choices and sabotaging your progress without you realizing it.

By questioning and overcoming these beliefs, you pave the way for personal and spiritual transformation. This involves identifying thoughts or patterns that no longer serve your purpose and replacing them with empowering beliefs that drive your growth. Cosmic Spirituality, in this context, invites you to expand your consciousness, freeing yourself from the limitations imposed by these beliefs and exploring new horizons of possibilities. By leaving these barriers behind, you can live more fully, aligned with your true potential.

Throughout your journey of expanding your consciousness, overcoming limiting beliefs plays a crucial role. These beliefs, as we have seen, are barriers that restrict your potential and distort your perception of reality. When identified and transformed, they become opportunities for you to expand your understanding of yourself and the cosmos, opening up space for practices that connect you with higher dimensions and your divine essence.

One of the most effective ways of dealing with limiting beliefs is through the regular practice of meditation, already discussed on previous pages. Meditation not only calms the mind, but also creates a state of receptivity that makes it easier to recognize and dissolve these beliefs. In this state of calm and inner connection, you can observe your thoughts and emotional patterns more clearly, allowing limiting beliefs to be identified and replaced with more positive and empowering perspectives.

By releasing the beliefs that bind you to a limited vision, you pave the way for practices such as astral projection. This experience goes beyond the limits of the physical body and provides a unique opportunity to explore subtle realms and higher dimensions. During astral projection, you can meet Beings of Light and spirit guides who offer profound insights and wisdom for your journey. This practice not only broadens your perception of the cosmos, but also reinforces the idea that your limitations are created by internal barriers that can be overcome.

As you venture into higher planes, the integration of self-knowledge with the expansion of consciousness becomes evident. Recognizing and working on your limiting beliefs is part of the process of delving into your inner self and confronting the deepest aspects of your psyche. This includes both light and dark traits, as both are essential for your spiritual evolution.

Transforming these beliefs is an indispensable step towards awakening your true essence. In doing so, you become increasingly aware of your connection to the cosmos and your multidimensional nature. From this state of expanded awareness, you realize that limiting beliefs are not just obstacles to be overcome, but also invitations to open up to new horizons, living in alignment with the wisdom and love of the universe.

Thus, overcoming limiting beliefs is not an end in itself, but an essential stage in your ongoing journey of self-discovery and expansion of consciousness. By integrating these transformations with spiritual practices such as meditation and astral projection, you strengthen your connection with the cosmos and access the true purpose of your existence.

10
Virtues and Values of the Beings of Light

In Cosmic Spirituality, the cultivation of virtues and values plays a fundamental role in the process of spiritual growth and the search for a full and meaningful life. The Beings of Light believe that these virtues and values are fundamental to the creation of a harmonious society, as well as to the elevation of collective consciousness.

One of the essential virtues cultivated in Cosmic Spirituality is compassion. Compassion is the ability to put yourself in the other person's shoes, to empathize and understand their pain and challenges. Compassion invites us to act with kindness and benevolence, recognizing the interconnectedness of all beings. By cultivating compassion, you expand your consciousness, promoting healing and harmony in your surroundings.

Another virtue valued by the Beings of Light is wisdom. Wisdom is the result of the continuous search for knowledge, experience and deep reflection. Wisdom allows us to perceive the truth and act with discernment in all situations. The search for wisdom involves a process of self-discovery and self-knowledge, in which you learn from your experiences and open up to a deeper understanding of life and yourself.

The Beings of Light value integrity as a fundamental virtue. Integrity involves acting in accordance with higher values; you need to be authentic and upright in your actions and words. It is the ability to keep your commitments and honor your promises. Cultivating integrity allows you to live according to your inner truth, establishing relationships of trust and respect with others.

Gratitude (as mentioned earlier) is also an essential virtue in Cosmic Spirituality. Gratitude is the invitation to recognize and appreciate life's blessings and gifts, even in challenging moments. It teaches you to value and express gratitude for every experience, person or opportunity that crosses your path. By cultivating gratitude, you open your heart to abundance and joy.

In Cosmic Spirituality, values also play a fundamental role in the journey of spiritual growth. Among the most important values of the Beings of Light is harmony. Harmony implies seeking balance between all areas of life, with the world around us. It is the search for inner peace and harmonious collaboration with others and with nature.

Another essential value is truth. The Beings of Light value the search for inner truth and authenticity in all actions. This involves living in alignment with your values and being honest with yourself and others. The search for truth helps you to grow and evolve spiritually, making a connection with your deepest essence.

Respect is a fundamental value in Cosmic Spirituality. Respect involves valuing and honoring the dignity of all beings, regardless of their differences. It is the recognition of equality and diversity as enriching aspects of life. By practicing respect, you contribute to building healthy relationships and creating a just and inclusive society.

Finally, the Beings of Light value love as the supreme value. Unconditional love is the force that permeates the entire universe, connecting all forms of life. Cultivating love in your heart and expressing it in action is the path to spiritual upliftment and personal transformation. Love is the connection with the Source, it is what enables a person to live with compassion, kindness and empathy.

By cultivating the virtues and values of the Beings of Light, you create a solid foundation for the spiritual journey and become an agent of positive transformation in the world. These values are a guide in the expansion of individual consciousness, connecting you with your highest essence and inspiring you to live in harmony with all beings and the universe.

11
The Transformative Power of the Cube of Light

On the path of the spiritual journey, there are various practices and techniques that help in the search for inner connection, the expansion of consciousness and energetic balance. One of these powerful practices is the Cube of Light, a tool that allows you to access and use high energies for personal transformation and conscious manifestation.

The Cube of Light is a symbolic representation of a multidimensional energy field that contains information and positive vibrations. It can be visualized and worked with mentally as a transparent, glowing, pulsating cube of light. Inside this cube, you find a sacred space where you can direct your intentions and carry out processes of healing, expansion and transformation.

When working with the Cube of Light, it's essential to establish a peaceful environment conducive to the practice.

Find a place where you feel comfortable and where there are no interruptions. Take a few moments to calm down and relax. Breathe deeply and allow your mind to quieten down.

Once you have reached a relaxed and meditative state, visualize a cube of bright light in front of you. Observe its shape, its colors and its luminosity. Feel the energy emanating from it, feel that it conveys a sense of peace, love and harmony.

As you connect with the cube's energy, move it, allowing it to envelop your whole being, filling it with light and positivity.

Inside the Cube of Light, you can carry out different practices and work with different intentions.

Healing and Transformation: When you enter the Cube of Light, you can direct your intention towards healing physical, emotional or spiritual aspects that need balance and harmony. Visualize yourself inside, seeing the light that fills all areas, dissolving blockages and promoting deep healing.

Conscious Manifestation: Use the Cube of Light as a sacred space to manifest your desires and dreams. Visualize your goals already achieved inside the cube, feeling the joy and gratitude for their materialization. Send this energy of manifestation out into the universe, trusting that the process of creation is underway.

Energetic Purification: Imagine yourself inside the Cube of Light, allowing its brilliant light to penetrate every cell of your being. Feel the light dissolving negative energies, transmuting limiting patterns and raising your vibration. Let the cube's light purify and renew you completely.

Spiritual Connection: Use the Cube of Light to connect with your Higher Self, spirit guides or Beings of Light. Visualize yourself inside the cube, opening yourself up to receive wisdom, guidance and inspiration. Be open to receiving messages or insights that arise during this connection.

As you regularly practice working with the Cube of Light, you strengthen your connection with cosmic energy, your inner wisdom and your ability to consciously create your reality. Remember that the cube is a powerful tool, but it is your intention and your conscious presence that activate and amplify its effects.

After each session of working with the Cube of Light, take a moment to express gratitude for the experience and the transformations that are manifesting in your life. Allow the cube's energy to continue to flow and expand, radiating out to the surroundings and the universe.

By incorporating the practice of the Cube of Light into your spiritual journey, you will be opening doors to self-development, to the conscious manifestation of your deepest desires and to the connection with higher dimensions of consciousness. Take advantage of this powerful tool and allow the Cube of Light to illuminate your path towards your divine essence.

Keep exploring, experimenting and deepening your relationship with the Cube of Light. Remember that the practice is a journey in itself, and every moment dedicated to this connection strengthens your bond with cosmic energies and your potential for conscious creation. Be open to the insights, learnings and blessings that this practice will bring to your life.

I invite you to enter into this experience with the Cube of Light and allow it to guide your journey of self-discovery, healing and transformation. Trust in your power and your ability to manifest the reality you desire. The light is within you, ready to shine and light the way.

12
Fundamentals of Cosmic Meditation

Meditation plays a central role in Cosmic Spirituality. It is an essential practice that allows you to enter into a state of deep connection with your inner being and with the subtle energies of the universe. Cosmic meditation is a powerful technique for expanding consciousness, increasing vibration and accessing higher levels of spiritual perception.

The fundamentals of Cosmic meditation are rooted in simplicity and focus of mind, although it has been explained on previous pages, for a better understanding of the chapter, I will describe another practical method of meditation.

To begin, find a quiet place where you can sit comfortably. It is preferable to choose a quiet environment where you feel connected to nature and can relax deeply.

Once you're in a comfortable position, close your eyes and start directing your attention to your breathing. Breathing plays an important role in Cosmic Meditation, as it helps to anchor the present moment, relaxing the body and mind. Breathe deeply, paying attention to the movement of air in and out of the body.

As you concentrate on your breathing, allow your mind to calm down. Notice the thoughts that arise, but don't get attached to them. Let them pass gently by, like clouds in the sky, turning your attention to the breath. The practice of observing thoughts without getting involved with them is a way of training the mind to become calmer and more receptive.

Once your mind has calmed down, you can begin to direct your attention to your inner self. Feel the presence of your essential self, your connection with Source and Cosmic consciousness. Allow yourself to feel a sense of peace, love and inner expansion. As you tune into this energy, you open up to receive insights, guidance and healing.

During Cosmic meditation, you can also visualize yourself in a cosmic environment. Imagine yourself in a place of beauty and peace, surrounded by beings of Light. Feel the loving and healing energy of these beings as they surround you with love and wisdom. Allow yourself to receive any messages or guidance that may arise during this visualization.

Cosmic meditation also involves using subtle frequencies and energies to raise your vibration and expand your consciousness. You can use positive affirmations, such as "I am light" or "I am love", while meditating to strengthen your connection with your divine nature. In addition, you can use crystals or symbols as energetic support during meditation.

Remember that the practice of meditation is personal and unique. There is no right or wrong way to meditate. The important thing is to take the time to connect with your inner essence, seeking peace and mental clarity, in order to receive the spiritual gifts that Cosmic Meditation offers.

As you delve deeper into your meditation practice, you will develop greater spiritual sensitivity, as well as a deep connection with the subtle realms of existence. This practice helps to expand your consciousness so that you can discover your true nature, aligning yourself with your spiritual mission on Earth.

13
Meditation for Connection with the Source

In Cosmic Spirituality, connecting with the Source is considered a fundamental quest. Source is the primordial energy, the cosmic consciousness from which all things originate. Connecting with this energy brings deep healing, wisdom and expansion of consciousness. You will learn some meditation techniques that help strengthen your connection with the Source of all things.

Conscious breathing meditation: Start by sitting comfortably and closing your eyes. Concentrate on your breathing, observing it as it enters and leaves your body.

As your mind calms down, direct your attention to the sensation of expansion that occurs with each inhalation and the sensation of release that occurs with each exhalation. Feel connected to the vital energy flowing through you, recognizing that this energy comes from the Source.

Sacred mantra meditation: Choose a mantra that resonates with you, such as "I am one with Source" or "I connect with Divine Source". Repeat the mantra allowing its words to create a powerful vibration within you. Focus on the intention behind the mantra and feel the energy of Source merging with yours. Let the mantra lead you into a deeper meditative state where you can experience a more intense connection.

White light meditation: Visualize a brilliant white light filling your entire being. Imagine this light as a direct manifestation of the Source, pure and sacred. Allow this white light to cleanse and purify your mind, body and spirit, dissolving any negative energy or blockages. Feel this loving light envelop you, allow it to strengthen your connection with Source.

Gratitude meditation: Gratitude is a powerful tool for connecting with Source. Take time to reflect on the blessings in your life and feel deep gratitude for them. As you meditate, focus on every aspect of life for which you are grateful, from the simplest things to the most significant. Feel how the Source is present in all these blessings and how gratitude expands your connection with this divine energy.

Open heart meditation: Imagine your heart opening like a blossoming flower. Visualize it filled with unconditional love and compassion. As you focus on the love in your heart, feel how this loving energy is connected to Source. Allow your heart to expand more and more, connecting deeply with the energy of Source, which is the pure essence of universal love.

When practicing these meditation techniques for connecting with Source, remember that the key lies in your intention. Be patient and persistent in your practice, allowing the connection with Source to deepen over time. Meditation is a personal and unique journey for everyone, and your experience with Source will be unique for you too.

14
Deepening the Connection

On the spiritual journey, seeking a deep connection with cosmic wisdom is essential. Cosmic wisdom is the understanding and knowledge that transcends the limitations of the human mind and originates from universal consciousness. It is an unlimited source of insight, clarity and guidance that helps you understand the true nature and purpose of your existence. We will explore ways for you to go deeper into this connection and this wisdom, learning to integrate it into your spiritual journey.

Inner silence: Cosmic wisdom often emerges from silence. Set aside time each day to be in silence, whether through meditation, contemplation or simply disconnecting from external noise. By allowing your mind to calm down and quieten down, you create space for cosmic wisdom to reveal itself. Be open and receptive to the subtle messages that arise during these moments of silence.

Connecting with nature: Nature is a portal to cosmic wisdom and part of its manifestation. By connecting with the natural world, you experience the harmony and order present in all of creation. Spend some time outdoors, observing the beauty of nature. Through this connection, you feel the deep interconnectedness with the universe and receive insights into cosmic wisdom.

Spiritual study: Seeking knowledge and wisdom through spiritual study is also a way of deepening your connection with cosmic wisdom. Read books, attend lectures, workshops or study the teachings of spiritual masters. These sources offer perspectives and insights that broaden understanding and awaken inner wisdom. Remember that spiritual study is not limited to theory, but is also linked to practice and direct experience.

Tuning in to intuition: Intuition is a direct channel to cosmic wisdom. By developing your intuitive capacity, you open yourself up to receiving insights and divine guidance. Practice inner silence and attentive listening, trust your feelings and be open to the subtle messages that arise in your consciousness. The more you trust your intuition, acting on its guidance, the deeper your connection with cosmic wisdom will be.

Energy connection practices: Energy is the vehicle that cosmic wisdom uses to flow. Practices such as energy channeling, creative visualization and energy healing open channels of communication with cosmic wisdom. By cultivating a conscious connection with universal energy, you access information and insights that transcend the limits of the rational mind.

Cultivating humility and detachment: Cosmic wisdom cannot be captured or controlled by the egoic mind. It is important to cultivate humility and detachment on your spiritual journey. Be open to recognizing that there is much more to be learned and understood beyond what you currently know. Allow yourself to let go of limiting beliefs and preconceived ideas, making space for cosmic wisdom to flow through you.

By deepening your connection with cosmic wisdom, you align yourself with the vastness of the universe and become a channel for divine expression. Remember that cosmic wisdom is not a goal to be achieved, but a continuous journey of discovery and expansion. Embrace this journey with gratitude and openness, trusting that cosmic wisdom will guide your path towards enlightenment and fulfillment.

15
Cosmic Starship Meditation

The Cosmic Starship Meditation is a powerful practice that allows you to experience the energy and consciousness of the Beings of Light in a profound and transformative way. This meditation transports you to the Cosmic Starship, where you connect with the Beings of Light by accessing their frequencies of love, healing and wisdom. Let's explore the steps to perform this meditation, knowing the benefits it brings to your spiritual journey.

Before starting the meditation, find a quiet space where you can sit comfortably. Turn off your electronic devices and take some time to relax and prepare yourself for this unique experience.

Start by breathing deeply and allowing your body to relax. Focus on letting go of any tension or worries you may be carrying. Visualize yourself surrounded by a protective, loving light that completely envelops you.

Set your clear intention to connect with the Beings of Light to receive guidance, healing and wisdom. Open your heart to receive the loving and benevolent energies that will be available to you during this meditation.

Visualize yourself entering a bright and luminous starship. Observe the details of the ship, such as colors, shapes and the serene atmosphere, enveloping yourself in this energy of peace and upliftment.

As you move around the ship, allow yourself to meet Beings of Light. They may present themselves as bright Beings of Light, with a loving and welcoming energy. Feel their presence around you and allow their energy to resonate with you.

In this sacred starship space, you can initiate telepathic communication with the Beings of Light. Ask questions, share your concerns, open yourself up to receive their answers and guidance. Feel enveloped by their cosmic wisdom and unconditional love.

Allow the energy of the Beings of Light to flow through you, bringing healing and transformation to whatever aspect of life you need help with. Feel this high energy penetrating your being, dissolving blockages, bringing balance and harmony.

At the end of the meditation, thank the Beings of Light for their presence and guidance. Feel grateful for the opportunity to connect with their energy and wisdom. Slowly bring your consciousness back to your physical body, feeling grounded and at peace.

The Cosmic Starship meditation is a personal and unique experience. As you practice regularly, you will notice an increase in mental clarity, feel a sense of inner peace and a greater connection with cosmic wisdom. Allow yourself to explore this practice and let it guide your journey of spiritual growth.

16
Integrating Meditation into Everyday Life

The practice of meditation is a powerful tool for cultivating inner peace, mental clarity and spiritual connection. However, you often face the challenge of integrating this practice into your busy everyday life. You will now learn strategies and tips for integrating meditation in a practical and meaningful way into your daily life, allowing you to reap the benefits of this transformative practice in all aspects of life.

Establish a meditation routine.

One of the most effective ways to integrate meditation into everyday life is to establish a routine. Set aside a specific time of day to sit and meditate. This could be in the morning, before you start your activities, or in the evening, before you go to sleep. Choose a time that works best for you and commit to following it regularly. This helps create a habit and makes meditation a natural part of your routine.

If you're short of time, start with short meditation sessions. Even a few minutes of mindful meditation can make a significant difference to your well-being. Take short breaks during the day, such as during a break at work or before a meal, to close your eyes, breathe deeply and connect with the present moment. These moments of conscious pause calm the mind, bringing clarity in the midst of everyday chaos.

Find quiet spaces.

Although it's ideal to have a space dedicated to meditation, this isn't always possible. However, you can find quiet spaces in your home or at work where you can retreat for a few moments of meditation. It could be a corner of your bedroom, a nearby park or even a quiet bathroom. The important thing is to find a place where you feel comfortable and can concentrate.

Practice meditation on the move.

Meditation doesn't just have to be about sitting in silence. You can integrate meditation into your daily activities, turning them into moments of mindfulness. For example, when walking, pay attention to the sensations in your body, the textures under your feet or your breathing. When you shower, feel the water touching your skin and concentrate on relaxing your body. When eating, savor the food, paying attention to the flavors and textures. These moving meditation practices help to bring mindfulness to all your daily activities.

Sometimes you can forget to meditate when you're involved in daily tasks. Use visual reminders, such as a reminder on your cell phone or a note that stays in a visible place. In addition, there are many meditation apps available that send notifications and offer different guided practices. These resources are useful for maintaining a regular and constant practice.

Another great way to integrate meditation into everyday life is to share the practice with others. This can be done by joining local meditation groups or even online, where you can connect with other practitioners and share your experiences. In addition, having an accountability partner or a friend with whom you can share meditation goals helps maintain commitment and motivation. By sharing your meditation journey, you create a sense of community and mutual support.

Meditation is an ancient practice that offers a number of benefits for the body, mind and spirit. Integrating meditation into everyday life brings about positive transformations in all aspects of life.

One of the most notable advantages of meditation is its ability to reduce stress and anxiety levels. By dedicating time to daily meditation, you calm your mind and reduce the activation of the sympathetic nervous system, which is responsible for the stress response.

This helps you cope better with challenging situations, increasing emotional resilience.

Meditation involves training the mind to focus on a single object or thought, such as breathing. This constant practice of concentration strengthens your attention span and increases mental clarity. As a result, you become more efficient in daily activities, make decisions with greater discernment and improve productivity.

By meditating regularly, you develop greater awareness of your emotions and thought patterns. This enables you to identify and deal with negative emotions in a healthy way, leading to greater emotional stability and overall psychological well-being.

Many people find it difficult to relax and switch off their mind before going to sleep. Meditation has been shown to be effective in promoting relaxation and reducing insomnia. Practicing meditation before bed prepares the body and mind for a peaceful and restful sleep.

By quieting the mind through meditation, you allow creativity to flourish and intuition to become more accessible. Innovative ideas and insights have more room to emerge when the mind is free of incessant thoughts and worries.

Studies have shown that meditation is associated with physical benefits, such as lowering blood pressure and the risk of cardiovascular disease. In addition, meditation strengthens the immune system, making the body more resilient to illness.

Meditation isn't just about individual benefits; it can also positively affect interpersonal relationships. By developing the ability to connect with yourself through meditation, you become able to understand yourself and relate better to others, cultivating empathy and compassion.

Meditation is a journey of self-exploration. By practicing it regularly, you become more aware of your thoughts, emotions and behaviors. This self-awareness allows you to identify limiting patterns and work to overcome them, favoring your self-development.

In short, integrating meditation into everyday life brings a series of tangible benefits, including better mental and physical health, increased mental clarity, emotional well-being, bringing more harmonious relationships to life. By establishing a meditation routine, finding quiet spaces or practicing meditation on the move, you enjoy these benefits in your daily life. Remember that meditation is an ongoing journey and that, with practice and patience, you will reap its rewards in all areas.

17
The Higher Self

In Cosmic Spirituality, understanding the Higher Self plays a fundamental role. The Higher Self is considered the highest part of consciousness, connected to the Divine Source and cosmic wisdom. Let's learn about the importance and aspects of the Higher Self in Cosmic Spirituality, as well as some practices for connecting and aligning with this essential part of your being.

From the Cosmic perspective, the Higher Self is the most authentic expression of who you really are. It is the connection with your divine nature and with cosmic consciousness. The Higher Self is pure love, wisdom and compassion, and has an expanded vision of existence beyond the limitations of the ego. It is the part of you that transcends the illusions of separation and recognizes the unity of all creation. Understanding and accessing the Higher Self is essential for the spiritual journey and personal evolution.

One of the main practices in Cosmic Spirituality is learning to recognize and listen to the voice of the Higher Self. It communicates through insights, intuitions, synchronicities and heightened feelings. It's either a soft, loving voice that guides you towards your life purpose and helps you make decisions in line with your true essence, or it's a warning of something imminent. Who hasn't had a strong feeling that manifested itself later? The answer to this question shows the presence of the Higher Self.

Another way to perceive the form of intelligence separate from your physical consciousness is to ask yourself if you can choose who you love, if you can choose which dish you like best, or if you can decide what you will or won't be afraid of. The answers to these simple questions indicate that there is another form of consciousness at work in you, one that is more subtle and intuitive, a voice that dictates patterns of behavior that are not subordinate to your physical consciousness.

But you can fine-tune your contact with this voice. To tune in to it, you need to cultivate inner stillness through meditation, reflection and silence, allowing the wisdom of the Higher Self to manifest in your consciousness.

Understanding the Higher Self is not limited to moments of meditation or specific spiritual practices. It is essential to integrate awareness of the Higher Self into all aspects of life. This means living in alignment with higher values, acting with love and compassion, cultivating gratitude and seeking the truth in all situations. When you become aware of the Higher Self's presence in every thought, word and action, you begin to live a more authentic, meaningful and fulfilling life.

Practices for Connecting with the Higher Self.

There are several practices in Cosmic Spirituality that help you connect and strengthen your bond with the Higher Self. Some of them include:

Meditation:

Set aside time each day to go inward, quiet your mind and open up to the presence of the Higher Self.

Self-inquiry:

Ask deep, reflective questions about your life, purpose and spiritual evolution, allowing the answers to flow from the Higher Self.

Creative Visualization:

Use visualization to connect with the wisdom and guidance of the Higher Self, creating mental images that represent your connection and alignment.

Love and Gratitude Practices:

Cultivate an open heart, practice acts of kindness and gratitude in your daily life, recognizing the Higher Self as the source of all love and abundance.

As you advance in your understanding of the Higher Self, you are able to live with greater clarity, authenticity and purpose. Recognize that you are a multidimensional being with a direct connection to the divine. Integrating the Higher Self into your spiritual journey leads to the expansion of consciousness and the manifestation of your true essence in the world.

18
Communication Techniques

In Cosmic Spirituality, communication with the Higher Self is an essential practice for seeking guidance, clarity and wisdom on the spiritual journey. Here are some powerful techniques for connecting and establishing a conscious dialog with your Higher Self. These techniques help with decision-making, personal development and alignment with your true essence.

Meditation is a powerful tool for establishing a deep connection with the Higher Self, as described on previous pages.

Automatic writing is the technique in which you allow your Higher Self to manifest itself through writing. Take a notebook and pen and start writing freely, without judgment or censorship. Let the words flow freely, allowing your Higher Self to express itself. You can start by asking a question or simply asking for guidance, then let the words flow naturally. This practice can be surprising and revealing, bringing deep insights and answers to your questions. Techniques for developing automatic writing are described on the previous pages.

Another way to communicate with your Higher Self is through a conscious internal dialog. Take a quiet moment and establish a mental dialog with your Higher Self. Ask questions and listen to the intuitive answers that arise in your consciousness. Remember that the Higher Self speaks in a loving and compassionate way, so be open to receiving answers that differ from your expectations. Don't be afraid, if you empty your mind and quieten your conscious you will clearly hear the voice of your Higher Self. Haven't you ever heard a voice that you don't know where it came from? Haven't you ever heard your name called while entering or leaving a state of vigilance before or after sleep?

The Higher Self often communicates through signs or synchronicities.

Synchronicities are significant and apparently coincidental events or happenings that occur in life, indicating a connection between the external world and our Higher Self. Look out for repetitive patterns, unexpected encounters, messages in dreams or any events that seem significant or symbolic. These signs can be interpreted as answers or confirmations from your Higher Self. Stay open and receptive to the signs that come your way and trust your intuition to interpret them.

Creative expression is also a powerful way of communicating with the Higher Self. Dance, music, painting or any art form that resonates with you opens up channels of subtle communication. Allow yourself to immerse yourself in these activities in a spirit of surrender and connection with the divine. Notice how creative expression releases blockages, raises your vibration and allows your true essence to manifest.

Remember that communication with the Higher Self is an ongoing practice and varies from person to person. Experiment with these techniques and find out which ones resonate best with you. Cultivate confidence in your ability to connect with the divine and be open to receiving the guidance and wisdom of your Higher Self. As you deepen your connection, you will be guided to a life that is more authentic, meaningful and aligned with your spiritual purpose.

19
Channeling and Messages

In Cosmic Spirituality, channeling is another practice that allows you to receive messages and guidance from Beings of Light. Through channeling, you access elevated information, profound insights and cosmic perspectives that help you on your spiritual journey and personal evolution.

Before starting the channeling process, it is important to establish a peaceful and sacred environment. Find a place where you feel comfortable and free from distractions.

Do a short meditation to center yourself and raise your vibration.

Visualize yourself surrounded by a protective and loving light, and ask for the presence and guidance of the Beings of Light in your channeling work. To facilitate channeling, tune in to cosmic energy. This can be done through visualization and intention.

Imagine yourself surrounded by a bluish light, similar to the color of the star Arcturus. Feel this energy penetrating your being and connecting with the wisdom and love of the Beings of Light. As you open up to this energy, allow it to flow freely through you as you prepare to receive messages.

Once you have established a connection with Cosmic energy, it's time to open up to channeling. This can be done in different ways, depending on your preferences and abilities. Some people prefer to write down the messages as they channel, others prefer to record their voices or even channel verbally. Find the approach that resonates most with you.

If you opt for written channeling, have a notebook or computer at hand. Start by writing a greeting to the Beings of Light, expressing your intention to receive messages. Then allow the words to flow freely, without judgment or censorship. Let your hand or fingers move intuitively, capturing the messages that are being transmitted. Trust the process and don't worry about coherence or grammar. Clarity and cohesion can be improved later.

If you prefer verbal channeling, find a quiet place where you can speak aloud without being interrupted. Begin the process by setting your intention and inviting the Beings of Light to share their messages through you. Start speaking freely, allowing the words to flow intuitively. You may feel a change in your voice, tone or even language and the way you express yourself. Trust in the wisdom that is being transmitted through you. It is recommended that you record the channeling, as some people achieve a deeper connection and go into a trance, later forgetting what was verbalized.

Once you have channeled the messages from the Beings of Light, it's time to interpret them. Read or listen carefully to what has been transmitted and allow yourself to feel the essence of the words. Observe insights, guidance or teachings that have been shared. Trust your intuition and the connection you have established with the Beings of Light. Remember that messages can come in the form of symbols, metaphors or images, and your personal interpretation is valuable.

Channeled messages from the Beings of Light are intended to help you on your spiritual journey and in your personal evolution. Consider how you can apply these messages in your daily life. Reflect on the insights you have received and how they can help you to grow personally, expanding your consciousness and living with more love, compassion and wisdom. Try incorporating the guidance into your meditation practices, the development of psychic abilities or your relationship with your Higher Self.

Channeling and receiving messages from Beings of Light is a wonderful way to expand your connection with the cosmos and receive valuable spiritual guidance. Remember to approach this practice with humility, love and respect, while maintaining the intention of serving the highest good. As you improve your ability to channel, your connection with the Beings of Light strengthens, providing a continuous flow of wisdom and enlightenment.

20
Spiritual Guidance and Personal Growth

On the spiritual journey, seeking guidance is a fundamental part of personal growth. Spiritual guidance helps to find clarity, purpose and direction in life, as well as deepening the connection with spirituality and the divine.

The first step in seeking spiritual guidance is crucial in the journey of self-discovery and personal growth. It is a moment of recognizing the need to look beyond oneself and seek answers and direction beyond what is immediately visible. This recognition often occurs when you find yourself lost, confused or misaligned about your purpose and path in life.

When you feel lost or disoriented, it's as if you're in a labyrinth, unable to find your way out on your own. At this point, it's important to have the humility to admit that you need help and that you can't always solve all your problems on your own. Seeking spiritual guidance is a demonstration of openness to receiving insights and external wisdom, whether through a spiritual guide, a mentor, a religious practice or even through connecting with nature and the energy of the universe. Seeking spiritual guidance in itself generates a change in the state of mind, opening the soul to receive subtle helping energies.

When you allow yourself to seek spiritual guidance, you are taking an important step towards a deeper understanding of yourself and your purpose in life. Spiritual guidance helps you to see beyond the superficial layers of existence; it is a connection with the deepest essence of your being.

In this search process, it is common to come across fundamental questions about who you really are, what the meaning of your existence is and how you could live more authentically and in line with your values and aspirations. Spiritual guidance helps you find answers by illuminating the path you need to take.

The search for spiritual guidance can take many forms, depending on individual beliefs and values. Some people may find inspiration through religious practices, while others may prefer to connect with nature, meditate or seek knowledge and wisdom in books and spiritual teachings. Regardless of the path you choose, spiritual guidance offers valuable support on your journey of self-discovery and growth. It helps you develop a deep connection with yourself, with other beings and with the universe as a whole. In times of difficulty, spiritual guidance gives you the strength to face challenges with greater courage and wisdom.

In Cosmic Spirituality, there are many sources of spiritual guidance available. You can seek the wisdom of the Beings of Light through channeling, as mentioned earlier. In addition, there are other forms of guidance you can explore, such as turning to spiritual mentors, spiritual guides, sacred books and meditative practices. Even your Higher Self can be a powerful source of knowledge and guidance.

Each of these sources of guidance brings a unique and valuable perspective that can help your spiritual growth. It's important to note that Cosmic Spirituality respects all forms of faith, whatever they may be. By referring to spiritual mentors or guides, the idea is that you can adapt these concepts to your own understanding of spirituality.

In this context, let's delve a little deeper into the sources of spiritual guidance linked to the Beings of Light.

Intuition.

In Cosmic Spirituality, intuition occupies a central place as a powerful tool for receiving spiritual guidance. It allows us to go beyond the limits of the rational mind, accessing information and insights that go beyond what can be perceived with the physical senses. Intuition is a bridge that connects you to divine wisdom and guides you towards choices and decisions in line with your spiritual path.

Developing and cultivating intuition is a valuable skill that you can hone. It's like tuning an instrument to pick up the subtle vibrations of the universe and hear its hidden melody. Through practice, you can tune your intuition so that it becomes a reliable compass on your spiritual journey.

Unlike the rational mind (which is based on past data and information), intuition operates in the present, connecting with the underlying energy and truth in a given situation. It is able to perceive nuances and details that escape the conscious mind, allowing you to make better decisions in tune with your deepest self.

Trusting your intuition is essential for receiving clear and authentic guidance. However, you can often be influenced by doubts and insecurities that obscure the clarity of your intuition. Practicing self-knowledge and meditation calms the mind, removing the interference that prevents you from hearing the inner voice.

In Cosmic Spirituality, intuition is considered a direct communication with the higher plane. Through it, you receive insights and messages from spiritual beings who guide and support you on your journey of personal growth. It's as if you were tuning into a cosmic radio station, picking up transmissions designed to help you on your evolutionary path.

In addition, intuition is also capable of alerting you to dangerous situations or guiding you to opportunities that may go unnoticed by the conscious mind. It's an inner voice that you shouldn't ignore, as it often offers a deeper and more comprehensive view of the circumstances you face.

However, it is important to remember that intuition is not infallible. It can be influenced by emotions and personal desires, and it is essential to combine it with discernment and common sense. Using intuition in conjunction with the rational mind allows for a balanced and complete approach to your decisions and choices.

Connection and Opening Practices.

Receiving spiritual guidance effectively requires a state of openness and receptivity. To cultivate this openness, you can incorporate specific practices into your daily life that will help you connect with spirituality, creating space to receive insights and guidance from the spiritual plane. Some of these practices include meditation, contemplation, prayer and sacred rituals, each of which plays a significant role in strengthening the spiritual connection.

Meditation.

Meditation (explained on previous pages) is one of the most powerful practices for achieving inner connection and spiritual openness. By silencing the mind and turning to the present moment, you open up space to access deeper levels of consciousness. Through meditation, you can quieten mental noise, release tensions and worries, and be receptive to receiving insights and messages from the universe. It helps you tune into your intuition and establish a deeper connection with your spiritual essence.

In addition to meditation, contemplation is another valuable practice for spiritual opening. By taking the time to reflect on life's essential questions, you can connect with deeper values and goals. Through contemplation, you can gain clarity about aspirations and challenges, as well as understand how they relate to your spiritual journey. This kind of self-examination makes you more receptive to receiving guidance that can direct your path.

Prayer.

Prayer is an extremely important and meaningful spiritual practice, as it is one of the ways to establish direct communication with the spiritual plane. By directing your prayers and intentions to a higher power, be it a deity, a spiritual guide or the universe itself, you open a line of connection that transcends the material plane and connects you with something greater than yourself.

Through prayer, you can express your longings, gratitude and deepest needs. It's a way of talking to the divine, of sharing your worries and hopes, your joys and sorrows. Prayer allows you to be authentic, because there is no judgment or limitations on feelings and words. It is a sacred space where you can express yourself fully, knowing that you are heard and understood.

Prayer also offers an opportunity for inner listening. By opening your heart and mind through prayer, you create a space to receive answers and guidance. These answers can come in different ways, whether through signs, synchronicities or insights sent from the spiritual plane.

Signs can manifest in subtle ways, such as unexpected events that seem to be connected to your prayers, or even in more obvious forms, such as an encounter with someone who offers a meaningful message. Synchronicities are coincidental events that seem to carry a special meaning, they help you realize that you are aligned with something greater than yourself. Insights, on the other hand, are profound ideas or understandings that spring from your own intuition and inner wisdom, and which often become more accessible after moments of prayer and reflection.

Through prayer, you can also nurture a sense of connection and purpose in life. By connecting with something bigger and higher, you find a sense of belonging to a greater whole, a feeling that you are part of a bigger and more meaningful plan. This gives comfort and courage, especially in times of difficulty.

It's important to remember that prayer goes beyond words. The attitude of an open heart and receptive mind during prayer is fundamental. Sincerity and faith put into prayers strengthen the connection with the spiritual plane, making the experience of prayer even deeper and more meaningful.

Sacred Rituals.

The Depth and Significance of Sacred Rituals in Spiritual Connection Sacred rituals play a prominent role in the search for spiritual connection and have been practiced in various cultures and traditions throughout history. Although they may vary widely according to beliefs and customs, they all have in common the essence of being symbolic expressions of connection with the sacred and the transcendent.

In essence, rituals are much more than mere repetitions of actions or empty ceremonies, they are ways of expressing devotion, reverence in the search for connection with higher forces, divine entities or the universe as a whole. Through sacred rituals, you transcend the material plane and enter a deep, spiritual dimension of existence.

One of the main characteristics of sacred rituals is their ability to raise consciousness. They create a special, sacralized space where you tune in to higher dimensions of your own spirituality. By getting involved in each stage of the ritual, whether through gestures, words or symbols, you open doors to more expanded states of consciousness. These moments allow you to transcend your everyday concerns by connecting with something that goes beyond the ephemeral, reaching the core of what is truly essential.

Another important function of sacred rituals is to create an atmosphere conducive to receiving spiritual guidance. Through them, you establish a channel of communication with the divine and tune in to cosmic wisdom. Rituals are like a bridge between the earthly plane and the spiritual plane, allowing you to approach the mysteries of existence while receiving valuable insights and guidance.

Sacred rituals don't have to be performed individually; many are practiced in community. The experience of participating in rituals together with other people creates a sense of belonging and union with something greater than yourself. This communal connection strengthens the spiritual experience and reminds us that everyone is interconnected on a spiritual journey.

It is essential to adapt the ritual practice to the form that resonates most with you. Some people prefer stillness, finding serenity the way they most identify with spirituality. On the other hand, other people benefit from the energy shared during collective rituals, feeling strengthened by the power of community. Cosmic Spirituality values the diversity of approaches and the importance of finding the spiritual path most aligned with your individual preferences and needs.

Sacred rituals encompass a wide variety of practices, from rites of passage and seasonal celebrations to healing and purification ceremonies. The choice of rituals depends on individual beliefs and traditions, and everyone can find meaning and purpose in their own ritual practices.

Spiritual practices:

Creating a routine of spiritual practices is a powerful way of nurturing the inner connection by attuning it to the deepest essence of being. By dedicating time and energy to these practices, you open up space to receive guidance and inspiration on your spiritual path.

One of the spiritual practices that can enrich your routine is keeping a spiritual diary. Writing down your thoughts, reflections and experiences in a journal allows you to process emotions and explore insights. By recording your intuitions and observing patterns in your life, you gain clarity about your personal and spiritual growth.

Another practice is to read inspiring spiritual texts. Books, articles or poems that address deep and meaningful themes inspire reflection on life, purpose and existence. These readings expand your understanding and connect you to ideas and concepts that resonate with your inner being.

Connecting with nature is also a valuable spiritual practice. By spending time outdoors, whether in a park, forest or beach, you reconnect with the beauty and harmony of nature. This connection helps you to feel part of something bigger, reminding you of the interconnectedness of all things.

Another spiritual practice that can be incorporated into your routine is practicing acts of kindness. By extending a helping hand to someone in need, you cultivate love and compassion in your heart. These altruistic actions connect you to the spirit of generosity and help create a more united and harmonious community. An excellent way to anonymously practice this kindness is through blood donation.

Blood donation is considered an act of kindness and generosity for several reasons. By donating blood, you are directly contributing to saving lives. Donated blood is used in a variety of situations, such as transfusions for patients undergoing surgery, medical treatment, serious accidents and for people suffering from diseases that require regular transfusions. Blood donation is an altruistic gesture, as you donate without expecting anything in return. It's a way of helping people you don't even know, which shows empathy and compassion for others.

Gratitude is also a simple and powerful spiritual practice. By taking a moment every day to express gratitude for the blessings in your life, you direct your focus to what is positive and abundant. This practice brings a sense of contentment and connects you to the source of joy within you.

By adopting a routine that includes these spiritual practices, you nourish your inner being and create a space conducive to receiving guidance and spiritual growth. These practices will remind you of your connection to the sacred and guide you towards self-discovery and the expansion of your spiritual awareness.

In short, the practices of connection and openness are fundamental to receiving spiritual guidance effectively. Through meditation, contemplation, prayer and sacred rituals and other practices discussed above, you connect with your spirituality, quieten the mind and create space to receive insights and guidance from the spiritual plane. These practices strengthen intuition and establish a deep connection with the spiritual essence, creating an environment conducive to receiving the guidance you seek.

When receiving spiritual guidance, it is essential to exercise discernment and authenticity. Not all guidance is appropriate, and it is important to assess whether it truly resonates with your essence and values. Discernment allows you to separate what is authentic and elevated from what is not, and you should trust your intuition and the wisdom of your heart when evaluating the messages you receive, always seeking the guidance that leads to the greatest personal and spiritual growth.

Remember that true spiritual guidance is not just about receiving insights and guidance, but also about applying them to your daily life. It is through practice that you experience growth and transformation. When receiving spiritual guidance, it is important to consider how you can incorporate these insights into your actions, relationships and choices. Spiritual guidance invites you to live according to the values and principles of Cosmic Spirituality, bringing peace, love and wisdom to the world.

By seeking spiritual guidance and working on your personal growth, you make room for the expansion of your consciousness and the manifestation of your highest potential. Guidance guides you towards your true essence and supports you on your spiritual journey. Remember that spiritual guidance is an ongoing process and that, as you open yourself up to receiving and applying this guidance in your life, you are constantly evolving and moving closer to your connection with the divine. Similarly, the practice of spirituality can be compared to the daily food given to a child, which makes it grow every day right under your eyes, even if you don't notice it. Just like a child who grows daily, your spiritual connection also develops gradually, even if this progress is not always immediately noticeable.

21
Co-creation with the Higher Self

Cosmic Spirituality recognizes you as a multidimensional being who has a direct connection with the Higher Self, your divine and eternal essence. Co-creating with the Higher Self is a powerful practice that allows you to manifest your true essence.

As explained earlier, the Higher Self is the highest and wisest part of your being, it is the direct connection to the divine and has a broad and deep understanding of your spiritual journey. Recognizing the Higher Self is recognizing that you are more than just a physical being, it is recognizing that there is a divine and accessible wisdom within you. It is an invitation to get in touch with this higher part of you and establish a conscious connection with it.

Co-creation with the Higher Self is a collaborative process between your earthly personality and your divine essence. It is recognizing that you have the power to manifest your reality and that you can do so in alignment with the will and wisdom of your Higher Self. Co-creation involves becoming aware of your thoughts, emotions and actions, always seeking alignment with the highest vision and purposes of your divine essence.

To co-create with the Higher Self, it is essential to cultivate a deep sense of alignment and trust. This means being in harmony with high values and purposes, acting in coherence with them. When you align with your Higher Self, you are open to receiving divine guidance and inspiration. Trust enables you to follow this guidance, even if you don't always fully understand why. It's believing that you are being guided to the best possible outcome.

There are various practices that strengthen connection and co-creation with the Higher Self. Just as prayer teaches us to seek peace, harmony and discernment through communication with a Higher Being, Cosmic Spirituality invites you to connect with your divine essence and use self-affirmation techniques aligned with the law of attraction.

Meditation (explained in previous chapters) is a powerful tool for silencing the mind and attuning it to the voice of your divine essence. During meditation, you can direct your intentions and desires towards the universe, using creative visualization to manifest your dreams and wishes.

Another way to strengthen the connection with the Higher Self is through conscious dialogue. You can ask questions and reflect on your intentions, seeking insights and guidance that come from your divine essence. This practice allows you to establish deep communication with the universe in order to receive answers and signs that will guide you on your path.

The practice of gratitude also plays a fundamental role in Cosmic Spirituality. Expressing gratitude for what you have and what you want to attract into your life is a powerful way of aligning your energy with the forces of the universe. By recognizing and appreciating the blessings present in your life, you create a state of abundance and openness to receiving even more.

Using positive affirmations is also a valuable technique for cultivating the co-creation mindset. By positively affirming your intentions and desires, you are reprogramming the subconscious mind while sending a clear message to the universe about what you want to manifest in your reality.

Therefore, by incorporating these practices into your spiritual journey, you are aligning concepts present in prayer and the law of attraction with the teachings of Cosmic Spirituality. By connecting with your Higher Self, expressing gratitude, using creative visualization and positive affirmations, you are consciously co-creating your reality, making room for the manifestation of your highest purposes and desires.

In co-creating with the Higher Self, it is important to practice letting go and being open to the opportunities and possibilities that arise along the way. This involves releasing rigid expectations and trusting that the universe is supporting your growth. Sometimes what you ask for may manifest differently than you imagine, but trust that the outcome is ideal for your growth and allow the magic of co-creation to flow.

Although co-creating with the Higher Self is a collaborative process, it is also important to remember that you are co-responsible for the manifestation of your reality. Taking responsibility for your choices, thoughts and emotions enables you to be conscious and intentional in co-creating. In addition, maintaining personal integrity, acting in alignment with values and principles, strengthens the connection with the Higher Self and supports the manifestation of your desires.

Co-creating with the Higher Self is an invitation to live an authentic, meaningful and purposeful life. As you connect with your divine essence and apply the principles of co-creation to your journey, you experience greater alignment with your true essence, manifesting the reality that reflects your highest vision. May this practice guide your path towards your unlimited potential and the full expression of your Cosmic essence.

22
Energetic Principles

In Cosmic Spirituality, it is necessary to understand that everything is energy and that you are constantly interacting with the vast energy field around you. In this context, it is important to explore the energetic principles that govern existence and consciously decide how to work with these energies to promote healing, balance and spiritual growth.

The first fundamental energetic principle is the recognition of the unity and interconnectedness of all things. From the Cosmic perspective, it is understood that all beings and objects are part of a vast web of interconnected energy. This means that your actions and intentions have the potential to affect not only you, but also the world around you. By honoring this interconnectedness, you become a conscious agent of positive change, promoting harmony and balance in your life and in the life of the planet.

Another important principle in Cosmic Spirituality is the understanding that everything in the universe has a unique vibration. Every thought, emotion or physical object emits a certain energy frequency. By tuning your vibration to a state of greater love, gratitude and compassion, you attract and manifest positive experiences in your life. This is because you are in resonance with energies of greater harmony and abundance. Aware of this principle, you can intentionally cultivate a high vibration and contribute to the creation of a healthier energetic environment.

Cosmic Spirituality is an approach that draws on the beliefs and teachings of a special civilization: the Arcturians. The Arcturians are evolved beings who inhabit the star Arcturus. They are conscious energy forms that reside in a higher dimension, known as the fifth dimension.

What makes the Arcturians so special is the fact that they have reached a high level of spiritual evolution, allowing them to access the "source of all things" - a powerful, universal force that some religions call God. They are considered to be guardians of cosmic wisdom and endowed with a deep connection to the universal energy that permeates the universe.

To form a mental image of the Arcturians Imagine them as ethereal beings, full of light and understanding, who transcend the limitations of space and time. Their heightened consciousness allows them to understand the deepest truths of the cosmos.

Within Cosmic Spirituality, Arcturians are seen as spiritual guides and mentors, assisting other life forms on their journey of growth and expansion of consciousness.

Although their existence is something beyond our physical comprehension, the Arcturians are considered a source of inspiration and wisdom, encouraging us to seek spiritual evolution and connection with the divine on our own path. This is the essence of Cosmic Spirituality and its vision of the beings who inhabit the star Arcturus.

From this point of view, understanding polarity is essential for spiritual development and advancing consciousness. According to the Cosmic perspective, all things in the universe are interconnected, interdependent, and polarity is a fundamental part of this interconnection.

Polarity is the manifestation of opposing dualities that coexist in all things. A classic example is the concept of yin and yang in Chinese philosophy, which represents the complementary duality of opposing forces, such as light and dark, positive and negative, expansion and contraction. These polarities are not only opposites, but also complementary, balancing each other out. In Cosmic Spirituality, this idea is applied more broadly to encompass all areas of existence.

To achieve a state of greater completeness and growth, Cosmic Spirituality encourages the integration and balance of these polarities. This implies accepting both the light and the dark within you, understanding that both are essential parts of the whole. It means recognizing the importance of balancing the masculine and feminine, regardless of gender, because both aspects are inherent in everyone.

In addition, Cosmic Spirituality teaches that the search for balance is not only internal, but also applies to relationships with the external world. It's understanding that every experience you have - both pleasant and challenging - has a purpose and offers opportunities for learning and growth.

By working to integrate these polarities through the prism of Cosmic Spirituality, you achieve a state of greater harmony, inner peace and expanded consciousness. This spiritual path involves a continuous journey of self-discovery, self-acceptance and learning in the quest to be in tune with the natural flow of the universe.

Although Cosmic Spirituality may not be widely known or accepted in all spiritual communities, for those who identify with this perspective, understanding polarity and seeking balance are valuable tools for enhancing the spiritual journey and connection with the universe as a whole.

The principle of intention and focus in Cosmic Spirituality is a powerful key to unlocking the creative potential that resides within you. This approach highlights the importance of being proactive in the direction of your desires and aspirations, consciously channeling your energy to create the reality you long for.

In essence, intention is the compass that points the way and shapes the spiritual journey. When you are clear about what you want to manifest in your life, you are attuned to the essence of your goals and dreams. By defining your intentions in a positive and meaningful way, you establish a deep connection with your inner purpose, bringing a higher meaning to everything you do.

However, intention alone is not enough; focus is just as vital. It is through focus that you concentrate your energies and efforts in the direction you choose to go. In a world full of distractions and external stimuli, the power of maintaining focus is truly transformative. When you allow yourself to be swept away by scattered thoughts or superficial distractions, your energy dissipates and the manifestation of your desires becomes more challenging.

Cosmic Spirituality guides you to cultivate the ability to remain centered and aligned with your goals, regardless of external circumstances. By maintaining clarity and firmness in your intention, you strengthen your connection with the universal flow of energy, allowing your creations to develop with greater fluidity.

Attunement with the universal flow is a fundamental aspect of the Cosmic approach. As you align your energy with the higher vibration of the universe, a powerful synergy is created that amplifies your intentions, creating a clear channel for the manifestation of your deepest desires.

However, it is important to remember that intention and focus must be combined with trust and surrender to the creative process. Sometimes reality can manifest differently than expected, but believing in the power of intention and being open to new possibilities allows you to recognize the universal flow and embrace the opportunities that come your way.

The essence of healing and energy transmutation in Cosmic Spirituality is an invitation to dive deep into your own essence, exploring and releasing energies that affect your balance and well-being. Your inner journey begins by recognizing that your past emotions, thoughts and experiences leave energetic imprints within you.

From this perspective, transmutation is the process of transforming and elevating these dense energies into higher, more positive frequencies, allowing healing and balance on all levels. It is the ability to release blockages and negative patterns, replacing them with higher energies, raising positive vibrations.

Energy healing practices, widely valued by the Beings of Light, are precious tools in the process of liberation and transmutation. Let's look at some of them from the point of view of transmutation.

Meditation, for example, is a portal to inner stillness, where you connect with your deepest essence. By allowing yourself to sink into the still waters of your mind, you identify and release energetic blockages that are holding you back in the past or disturbing your present peace.

Visualization is another transformative practice, which allows you to create mental images of healing and renewal. By projecting your mind into a positive scenario, visualizing yourself full and balanced, you accelerate the healing and transmutation process. Visualization is a powerful ally for dissolving negative energy patterns and replacing them with elevated, positive energies.

Energetic healing and transmutation are not just limited to the individual dimension; they also have the power to affect your connection with the world around you. As you heal internally, you also contribute to collective healing. Your transformed energies radiate beyond you, touching the lives of those around you, contributing to the creation of a higher vibration in your environment.

The process of energy healing and transmutation is continuous and requires dedication and self-compassion. As you go deeper into your healing journey, you will find deep layers of emotions and beliefs that need attention and release. In this process, it is essential to be gentle with yourself and allow yourself to feel and release whatever is necessary to promote deep and lasting healing.

By embracing the principle of energy healing and transmutation in Cosmic Spirituality, you are invited to become a guardian of your own energy, working diligently to create a state of balance and harmony in all aspects of your being. As you open up to healing, you align with your true essence and become a co-creator of a brighter and more loving reality, both for yourself and for the world around you.

Another technique is Flow and Acceptance.

The principle of flow and acceptance teaches you to flow with the energies of the universe instead of resisting them. It's important to recognize that life is a journey of constant change and that not everything is under your control. By cultivating a posture of acceptance and openness, you allow energy to flow freely in your life, facilitating growth, transformation and the manifestation of your highest potential.

By understanding and applying these energetic principles to your spiritual journey, you expand your consciousness, deepen your connection with the Higher Self and create a reality aligned with the Cosmic essence. Energy is a powerful tool that you have at your disposal. By using it wisely, you unlock the mysteries of the universe and awaken your unlimited potential.

23
Energy Alignment Exercises

You will now explore some energy alignment exercises practiced in Cosmic Spirituality. These exercises aim to promote balance, harmony and the expansion of consciousness, allowing you to tune in to universal energy and connect deeply with your Higher Self. Here are some practices you can incorporate into your daily routine to strengthen and balance your energy field.

Before diving into energy alignment exercises, it's important to get to know the chakras. The chakras are energy centers located along the spine, each corresponding to different aspects of physical, emotional, mental and spiritual life. Briefly explore each one, its location and corresponding color.

Root Chakra (Muladhara)

Located at the base of the spine, in the coccyx region, this chakra is associated with survival, security and connection with the earth. Its color is red.

Sacral Chakra (Swadhisthana)

Located below the navel, this chakra is related to creativity, pleasure and emotional expression. Its color is orange.

Solar Plexus Chakra (Manipura)

Located in the stomach area, this chakra is related to personal power, self-esteem and self-confidence. Its color is yellow.

Heart Chakra (Anahata)

Located in the center of the chest, this chakra is associated with love, compassion and emotional connection. Its color is green.

Throat Chakra (Vishuddha)

Located in the throat, this chakra is related to communication, expression and truth. Its color is sky blue.

Third Eye Chakra (Ajna)

Located between the eyebrows, this chakra is associated with intuition, wisdom and mental clarity. Its color is indigo (navy blue).

Crown Chakra (Sahasrara)

Located at the top of the head, this chakra is related to connection with the divine, spirituality and expansion of consciousness. Its color is violet or white.

Energy Center Meditation.

Energy center meditation is a powerful practice for connecting to these centers. Start by sitting comfortably in a quiet place.

Close your eyes and bring your attention to your breathing. Next, visualize a white or golden light coming out of the top of your head and traveling throughout your body, gently penetrating each chakra, from the crown chakra to the root chakra.

Feel the light vitalizing and balancing each energy center as it passes through them. Remain in this visualization for a few minutes, allowing yourself to feel the harmony and integration throughout your being.

Energy Cleansing with the Violet Flame.

The violet flame is a transmutation and energetic cleansing tool widely used in Cosmic Spirituality. This practice aims to release negative energies, transmuting them into light and love.

Sit in a quiet space and visualize yourself surrounded by a bright violet flame.

Allow this flame to penetrate your energy field, dissolving any blockages, limiting thoughts or dense emotions. Imagine the violet flame transmuting these energies into light and releasing them into the universe. Feel increasingly lighter, purified and aligned with the Cosmic energy of love and healing.

Conscious Breathing.

Conscious breathing is another simple and powerful practice that helps you tune into the present moment and your own energy. Find a quiet place where you can sit comfortably.

Close your eyes and pay attention to your breathing.

Breathe deeply through your nose, filling your abdomen and chest with air. Then exhale slowly through your mouth, releasing any tension or worry. As you continue to breathe consciously, allow your breathing to become smooth, fluid and rhythmic.

Feel how the vital energy flows in sync with your breath, nourishing and balancing your being. You can imagine purifying smoke being inhaled while denser smoke is exhaled, feeling that each exhalation is a cleansing process. While the pure smoke, which represents the good energies, enters through the aspiration and settles in your being, the dense smoke leaves your body, heading towards the vast universe.

Creative Visualization.

Creative visualization is a powerful practice for consciously directing energy and manifesting desires and intentions.

Choose a goal or intention you want to manifest and create a vivid image in your mind.

Visualize yourself already living that reality, feeling the positive emotions associated with it. As you visualize, allow your energy to align with the desired reality, expanding to embody it fully.

Feel connected to the Cosmic energy of wisdom, love and manifestation as you carry out this practice. Trust in your ability to co-create reality and allow the universal energy to work in harmony with you.

Cosmic Energy Bath.

A cosmic energy bath is a simple and relaxing practice that allows you to absorb and integrate the healing and harmonious energies of the Beings of Light.

Fill a bathtub with warm water and add a few drops of lavender or eucalyptus essential oil to further promote relaxation.

As you get into the bath, imagine yourself immersed in a white or golden light that bathes your whole being.

Feel the cosmic energy penetrating deep into your energy field, cleansing, healing and strengthening you. Allow yourself to relax and absorb this energy for as long as you wish, and feel refreshed and balanced after the energy bath.

These energy alignment exercises are just some of the practices that can be incorporated into your spiritual journey. By practicing them regularly, you strengthen your connection with your Higher Self, expanding your awareness and promoting balance and harmony in all aspects of your life.

24
Healing and Balance

Let's explore the incredible capacity for healing and balance that energies provide in Cosmic Spirituality. As you expand your awareness and connect with the energies of the universe, you can access a powerful flow of healing and transformation. It's time to explore some practices and concepts related to healing and balance through cosmic energies.

In Cosmic Spirituality, all forms of healing have their origin in the Source, the Source is the primordial energy of the universe. By recognizing yourself as a being interconnected to this Source, you make room to receive the cosmic energies of healing and balance. You can do this through intention, meditation and a deep connection with your own divine essence. By recognizing the Source as the first source of all things, you become a channel for transformative energies.

To access the cosmic energies of healing and balance, it is important to tune in to them. You can do this through meditation, visualization and intention. Although the topic of "meditation" has been covered previously, it is important to put it into context from the point of view of healing, as this practice can be used to help people who are not aware of Energy Healing methods. In these situations, you are the healing agent, the one who carries love and solidarity, acting within the principles of Cosmic Spirituality.

To access the cosmic energies of healing and balance in a specific and targeted way, it is possible to adapt the visualization according to the specific illness a person is facing. Visualization is a powerful tool for interacting with healing energy and directing it to the specific areas of the body that need attention.

For example. If you or someone you need to help is dealing with an illness, such as chronic pain in a part of the body or a specific condition, you can follow this visualization process during meditation.

Find a quiet, comfortable place to meditate.

As before, close your eyes and begin the relaxation process taught on previous pages.

When you reach a state of relaxation, focus on the area of the body affected by the illness. Visualize this part of the body as a sphere of energy, it can have a specific color, according to your intuition.

Imagine a radiant, healing cosmic golden light flowing from the universe directly into the palm of your hands.

Place your hands on the affected area, visualizing the golden light being transferred to the sphere of energy that represents the illness.

While keeping your hands on the area, visualize the golden light enveloping and penetrating the sphere, radiating warmth and a sense of healing and balance.

Remain in this visualization, allowing the cosmic healing energy to act on the affected area, bringing relief, relaxation and a sense of renewal.

Thank the cosmic energies for the healing and continue breathing deeply to fully integrate the experience.

It's important to note that visualization is a personal practice and can vary from person to person. The most important thing is that you feel connected to the energy and confident in your approach to assisting the healing process of a specific illness.

Energy Ray Healing is a spiritual practice that is deeply valued in Cosmic Spirituality. The rays are channels of divine energy that flow through the universe, bringing specific qualities of healing, balance and transformation to all dimensions of existence. Each cosmic ray is represented by a color and carries a distinct quality associated with it.

The Blue Ray is a symbol of healing and protection. By attuning to this ray, it is possible to access a regenerating energy that dissolves blockages, clears dense energies and provides a sense of serenity and protection all around. Visualizing the Blue Ray enveloping the body during meditation is a powerful way of allowing this healing energy to flow through the whole being, working on subtle and deep levels to restore balance and harmony.

The Pink Ray is the representation of unconditional love and compassion. By immersing yourself in the energy of the Pink Ray during meditation, you open your heart to a deeper and more compassionate love, both for yourself and for others. This gentle, caring energy heals emotional wounds and strengthens bonds of connection with the world around you, nurturing relationships and bringing a sense of unity and harmony.

The Golden Ray is the expression of wisdom and spiritual enlightenment. Visualizing the Golden Ray during meditation is a journey in search of elevated knowledge and mental clarity. This brilliant energy brings insights and inspiration, allowing you to understand complex issues with greater discernment and integrity. By attuning to the Golden Ray, you expand your consciousness and connect with inner wisdom, becoming a channel for spiritual enlightenment.

The Green Ray of Healing is an energy channel that represents the renewal and restoration of physical, emotional and spiritual health. To tune in to this ray during meditation, you visualize a green light enveloping and penetrating all the parts of your being that need healing. This revitalizing green energy works to balance the body and mind, providing a sense of well-being and vitality.

The Violet Ray of Transmutation is a transformative energy that brings purification and the release of negative patterns. To incorporate the Violet Ray during meditation, you can visualize it as a violet light that dissolves any dense energy, past karmas or limiting thoughts. This alchemical energy allows you to free yourself from emotional and spiritual baggage, making room for growth and evolution.

The White Ray of Purity is a divine energy that represents the connection with the Higher Self and spiritual wisdom. To visualize the White Ray during meditation, you can tune into the purest essence of your being, allowing the white light to penetrate all layers of consciousness. This illuminating energy brings clarity, inner peace and a sense of oneness with the divine.

The Yellow Ray of Enlightenment is an energy channel that represents the expansion of consciousness and the search for higher knowledge. To connect with this ray during meditation, you can visualize it as bright yellow light radiating wisdom and insights into spiritual and philosophical matters. This yellow energy stimulates the mind, awakening its ability to discern and understand deeper aspects of existence.

The Orange Ray of Creativity is an energy that inspires creative expression and connection with the power of the imagination. By tuning into this ray during meditation, you can visualize a vibrant orange light activating your inner creativity. This orange energy stimulates the ability to manifest new ideas, projects and innovative solutions in your life.

The way you visualize these rays is also important within Cosmic Spirituality: you can visualize yourself being bathed in the ray's light or being struck by it. Both approaches are valid and can be used according to personal preference and intuition. The effectiveness of the practice is not restricted to just one form of visualization, and both forms can bring significant benefits. Let's explore both options further.

Light Bath Visualization:

In this approach, the person visualizes herself immersed and bathed in the light of the specific cosmic ray. They can imagine this light flowing from top to bottom, enveloping their entire body and energy field. This visualization can be especially useful for those seeking the sensation of deep immersion in the energy of the cosmic ray, as if they were diving into its healing and transforming essence.

This visualization allows the person to feel enveloped and nourished by the energy of the cosmic ray, providing a sense of total connection with this healing frequency. The experience can be compared to taking a bath in purifying light, where all areas of the being are permeated by this revitalizing energy.

Visualization of Receiving the Universe.

In this approach, the person opens up to receive the energy of the cosmic ray that flows directly towards them from the universe. They can imagine themselves with open arms and an open heart, allowing the energy of the cosmic ray to enter their being. This visualization can be especially powerful for those who wish to experience a more direct connection with universal power and the divine aspect of cosmic ray energy.

This visualization allows the person to feel receptive and open to receiving the cosmic ray energy as a gift from the universe. It is a practice of surrender and trust, where you give yourself over to the healing wisdom of the ray, allowing it to work in your being in a harmonious and transformative way.

Both forms of visualization are highly effective and can be alternated or combined according to individual preference. The important thing is for the person to feel comfortable and in tune with the experience, allowing the energy of the cosmic ray to flow freely in their being, bringing healing, balance and expansion of consciousness. By practicing visualization with intention, faith and surrender, you will experience profound and positive results in your journey of self-discovery and spiritual growth.

By practicing Healing through the Cosmic Rays, you open a channel to divine wisdom and become a co-creator of your own healing and spiritual evolution. This practice is an opportunity to connect with the vast universe of subtle energies, reminding you that you are a spiritual being living a human experience with the power to access and use the energies for healing, for your own well-being or that of people who are less spiritually enlightened.

Harmonizing with the Stars and Asters is another practice deeply rooted in Cosmic Spirituality, where they possess subtle energies that influence and assist in the healing process. You can connect with these energies through observation of the celestial bodies, meditation and intention. By observing the beauty of the starry sky, you become aware of your connection with the universe and allow the stellar energies to flow into your being, bringing balance and renewal. In addition, you can use crystals or stones related to the stars to amplify and focus these cosmic energies.

During meditation, you can deepen your connection with the stars. Visualize your energy expanding beyond the physical body by connecting with the vastness of the cosmos. In doing so, you allow the stellar energies to flow into your being, bringing a sense of alignment and harmonization with stellar wisdom.

Remember the importance of intention in this process. By setting the intention to connect with the stellar energies in order to receive their healing blessings, you open a channel for the transmission of these energies into your life. This conscious intention strengthens your attunement with the universe and allows you to receive its beneficial influences.

Harmonizing with the Stars and Asters in Cosmic Spirituality is intrinsically linked to the particularities of the human condition and the subtle and significant influence that certain stars and asters have on us. In this practice, stars can be associated with planets that play important roles in your life, while stars represent broader cosmic energies that transcend your earthly existence.

In Cosmic Spirituality, some of the stars that resonate with the particularities of the human condition are:

The Sun:

To understand Cosmic Spirituality, the question of the Sun needs a broader explanation. It is seen as a central star that goes beyond its physical role as the provider of light and life on Earth. It represents a powerful source of vital energy, spiritual enlightenment and inner strength. Tuning in to the Sun's energy is a significant spiritual practice, as it brings profound benefits to the human being, who needs to understand that their life exists because the sun exists.

Solar energy is associated with the Higher Self, the highest and most spiritual aspect of the individual. By connecting with this energy, you experience greater mental clarity, which helps to dispel confusion and uncertainty. In addition, strengthening the connection with the Higher Self allows you to access the source of inner wisdom in order to gain a deeper understanding of your purpose in life.

Just as the Sun is the source of life on Earth, from the perspective of Cosmic Spirituality, solar energy is seen as the basis for spiritual life cycles. The sun's rays are the symbolic representation of the light that illuminates the individual's spiritual path, providing growth, evolution and continuous renewal. They nourish not only the physical body, but also the spiritual body, stimulating spiritual development and the awakening of consciousness.

When you tune into solar energy, you experience a sense of purpose and authenticity, as you align yourself with your true inner essence and the source of your life. This connection with the Sun's life force also brings a deep sense of vitality and enthusiasm for life, encouraging you to pursue your goals with determination and confidence.

Within the intricate system of Cosmic Spirituality, the Sun is a fundamental point for understanding the connection between cosmic energy and the human experience. It is one of the primary sources of energy that influence and shape existence. By honoring and aligning with this energy, you access a vast spiritual potential and open up to a universe of possibilities for growth, understanding and healing.

The Moon:

The Moon exerts a strong influence on emotions and natural cycles. It is associated with intuition, creativity and feminine energy. By harmonizing with lunar energy, you explore the depths of your emotions and access the intuitive wisdom that resides within you.

Mercury:

In harmonizing with the planet Mercury, you can connect with the energy of communication, expression and the analytical mind. Harmonizing with Mercury enhances communicative skills, clarity of thought and the search for knowledge.

Venus:

Venus is the planet of love, beauty and harmony. By attuning to Venus' energy, you cultivate unconditional love for yourself and others, and attract relationships and experiences that promote harmony and compassion.

Mars:

In harmonizing with the planet Mars, you access the energy of action, determination and courage. This harmonization boosts your motivation and your ability to face challenges, enabling you to move forward on your journey with confidence.

Alpha Centauri Stars:

In Cosmic Spirituality, the Alpha Centauri stars are considered special connections with Cosmic energies. Harmonizing with these stars amplifies the connection with cosmic wisdom, stimulates expanded consciousness and opens portals to spiritual healing.

Use crystals and gemstones to enhance harmonization with the stars. Each crystal has a unique energy and is associated with specific planets or stars. Place these crystals around the body during meditation or use them in jewelry, or amulets to attract and anchor the stellar energies in your daily life.

Sun:

The crystals associated with the Sun are Citrine and Topaz.

Citrine is known for its solar energy, this crystal brings joy, vitality and mental clarity. It is an element that strengthens the connection with the Higher Self, bringing light to the spiritual path.

Topaz is associated with the power of the Sun, helping to increase self-confidence, bringing courage to face challenges, making you move towards your life purpose.

Moon:

The crystals associated with the Moon are Rose Quartz and Moonstone.

Rose Quartz represents unconditional love and is a crystal that harmonizes emotions and nurtures relationships, opening the heart to compassion and connection with one's inner self. Moonstone strengthens intuition and sensitivity, it is a crystal that allows you to explore the depths of emotions and access intuitive wisdom.

Mercury:

The crystals associated with Mercury are Blue Agate and Sodalite.

Blue Agate facilitates clear and effective communication, helping to express ideas and thoughts objectively and calmly. Sodalite stimulates the analytical mind, helps in the search for knowledge, promoting discernment and understanding of situations.

Venus:

The crystals associated with Venus are Green Quartz and Desert Rose.

Green Quartz connects you with love and healing, attracts harmony to relationships and stimulates an open heart. Desert Rose strengthens self-esteem and inner beauty, and also promotes peace and serenity.

Mars:

The crystals associated with Mars are Garnet and Carnelian.

Garnet strengthens willpower and physical energy, boosting action and the ability to overcome obstacles. Carnelian stimulates courage and motivation, helps to face challenges and move forward with confidence.

Alpha Centauri stars:

The Alpha Centauri stars are considered special in Cosmic Spirituality. For this connection, there is no specific crystal, but clear crystals, such as transparent quartz or white quartz crystal, are used to amplify the connection with Cosmic energies.

By exploring harmonization with the stars, you open yourself up to a journey of personal discovery and connection with the universe. Using practices such as observation, meditation and intention, you align yourself with these cosmic energies, allowing them to flow into your being, bringing balance, renewal and spiritual growth. By nurturing your connection with the stars, you strengthen your spiritual journey and become a conscious co-creator of your own evolution.

Working with Healing Frequencies is a deeply transformative journey that you can explore in your spiritual practice. The sound vibrations present in healing frequencies have the power to balance and harmonize your being on subtle levels, promoting a state of well-being and connection with cosmic wisdom.

One of the most powerful techniques you can use is the use of mantras. By repeating healing mantras, you allow these sacred words to reverberate in your being, creating a field of positive and transformative energy around you. Mantras have the power to unblock stagnant energies, releasing any tension or blockages that may be affecting your emotional and spiritual balance.

Chants also play a significant role in working with healing frequencies. By allowing your voice to express itself through chants and vocalizations, you release stuck energies, creating a space of renewal and harmony. The voice is a powerful instrument for transmuting energies and connecting you with the essence of your authentic self.

Therapeutic music is another valuable tool you can use to work with healing frequencies. Music specially designed for this purpose has the power to calm the mind, relax the body and uplift the soul. These carefully selected melodies create an environment conducive to healing, opening the heart to receive blessings from cosmic energies.

By allowing the healing frequencies to penetrate your being through these practices, you open yourself up to a profound journey of transformation and balance. Healing manifests on all levels of being: physical, emotional, mental and spiritual. Remember that healing is an ongoing process, and working with healing frequencies is a powerful way to strengthen your connection with the universe, nurturing the divine essence that dwells within you. By incorporating these techniques into your routine, you become a channel for healing, allowing the wisdom of the universe to flow through you, bringing balance, renewal and harmony to life.

25
Energy Centers

The chakras (mentioned earlier) are energy vortices located in the body and play a vital role in physical, emotional and spiritual health. They act as energy channels that absorb, process and distribute vital energy throughout the being. Cleansing and harmonizing these energy centers is essential for balance and well-being. Let's explore some of the practices and techniques used in Cosmic Spirituality to cleanse and harmonize the chakras.

Although each of the chakras has been described previously, for didactic purposes, we're going to delve deeper into the subject from the perspective of their energetic cleansing and harmonization.

First, however, it is important not only to get to know each of these energy centers, but also to understand their relationship with aspects of life.

As mentioned above, the chakras are located along the spine, from the base to the top of the head, and each one is associated with a color, a function and specific aspects of human existence.

Root Chakra (Muladhara):

Located at the base of your spine, in the lower lumbar region, at waist level, it is associated with security, stability and connection with the earth. Its color is red. It influences survival, a sense of belonging and solid foundations. The light from the Root Chakra projects from the back, rooting it firmly to the earth, allowing the person to feel safe and secure. The mantra associated with this chakra is "LAM". It helps strengthen the connection with the earth and promote stability and security in life.

Sacral Chakra (Swadhisthana):

Located in the region below your navel, the Sacral Chakra is related to sexuality, creativity and vital energy, its color is orange and it influences emotional expression, pleasure and fertility. The mantra associated with this chakra is "VAM".

Solar Plexus Chakra (Manipura):

Located in the stomach region, the Solar Plexus Chakra is related to personal power, self-confidence and the manifestation of goals, its color is yellow and it influences willpower, self-esteem and the ability to make decisions. The associated mantra is "RAM".

Heart Chakra (Anahata):

Located in the center of your chest, the Heart Chakra is related to love, compassion and harmony, its color is green or pink and it influences interpersonal relationships, forgiveness and unconditional love. The associated mantra is "YAM".

Laryngeal Chakra (Vishuddha):

Located in the throat, the Laryngeal Chakra is associated with communication, personal expression and verbal creativity, its color is light blue and it influences the ability to express the truth, authenticity and clarity of communication. The associated mantra is "HAM".

Third Eye Chakra (Ajna):

Located between the eyebrows, the Third Eye Chakra is related to your intuition, inner wisdom and spiritual perception, its color is indigo (navy blue) and it influences intuition, imagination and the ability to visualize. The mantra associated with this chakra is "OM" or "AUM".

Crown Chakra (Sahasrara):

Located at the top of your head, the Coronary Chakra is related to spirituality and the connection with the divine, its color is violet or white and it influences the connection with the higher self, transcendental wisdom and the search for enlightenment. The associated mantra is "OM" or "AUM".

By chanting or repeating the mantras, you direct energy to the specific chakra, helping to balance it and open up pathways for vital energy to flow freely through the energy system. Remember that the correct pronunciation and chanting of the mantras is important to get the maximum benefit.

By associating the function and colors of each chakra with your mantras, you can work to balance, cleanse and purify them in order to strengthen their vital energy, promoting a more harmonious and fulfilling life in all aspects.

There are various practices you can use to cleanse and purify the chakras. One common technique is visualization, in which you have to imagine a bright, purifying light corresponding to the color of the chakra bathing it, removing blockages and stagnant energies while chanting your mantra. You can start at the base of the spine and work your way up, concentrating on each chakra individually. As you visualize the purifying light, and chant mantras related to each chakra, you strengthen the intention of cleansing and harmonizing. In addition, the practice of meditation, conscious breathing, herbal baths and crystals also help to cleanse the chakras.

After cleansing the chakras, it is important to seek balance and harmonization in these energy centers. Each chakra has a specific vibratory frequency and when they are out of balance they cause physical, emotional and spiritual problems. To promote harmonization, you can use techniques such as chakra meditation, in which you concentrate on each chakra in order to restore the balanced flow of energy. You can also use associated colors, sounds, crystals and essential oils.

Cleaning and harmonizing the chakras are practices that should be incorporated into your routine. Just as you take care of your physical and emotional body, you should also take care of your energy and your energy centers. This involves becoming aware of your thoughts, emotions and actions, seeking integrity and authenticity in all areas of life. In addition, dedicating time regularly to practices such as meditation, conscious breathing, visualizations and other chakra cleansing and harmonization techniques helps to maintain a state of balance and well-being.

Cleansing and harmonizing the energy centers is fundamental to health and spiritual growth. By working with the chakras, you unblock the flow of energy, promote healing, strengthen the connection with the divine and expand consciousness. Remember that you are unique, so adapt these practices to your intuition and personal needs. By cultivating chakra cleansing and harmonization, you are nourishing your whole being, allowing your energy to flow freely, enabling you to live a full and meaningful life.

26
Energetic Alignment and Lifestyle

Learn about the importance of integrating energy alignment with lifestyle in Cosmic Spirituality.

You've learned about the concepts of energy, chakras, meditation and techniques for cleansing and harmonizing the energy centers, now it's time to understand how you can incorporate these teachings and practices into your daily life, transforming them into a holistic and integrated lifestyle.

Energetic Awareness.

The first step to integrating energetic alignment into your lifestyle is to develop constant energetic awareness. This means being aware of your own energies, emotions and thoughts, observing how they affect your general well-being. Throughout the day, take a few moments to connect with your inner energy, observe your emotions and identify possible blockages or imbalances. This practice of self-observation allows you to become more aware of the areas that need attention and care. However, many people find it difficult to establish evaluative criteria and identify blockages and imbalances.

In a didactic way, we can say that energetic awareness is an essential practice for identifying blockages and imbalances in your daily life. To develop this awareness, you can follow a few simple steps.

Throughout the day, take a few moments to pause and connect with yourself. It could be a short break between tasks, a few minutes of meditation or even a quiet walk in nature. These moments of pause allow you to tune into your inner energy and observe how you are feeling.

Pay attention to your emotions throughout the day. Identify whether you are feeling happy, sad, stressed, anxious, etc. Emotions are powerful indicators of the state of your internal energy and can point to possible blockages or imbalances. Each emotion has a unique energetic resonance that reflects how you are relating to yourself and the environment around you. Emotions are linked to the chakras and changing your emotional state requires energetic cleansing and alignment of the corresponding chakra with the techniques taught on previous pages. Here are some common emotions that are indicators of blockages or imbalances.

Joy:

Joy is a positive emotion that indicates that your energy is flowing harmoniously. Feeling joyful usually suggests a healthy balance between your physical, emotional and spiritual aspects.

Sadness:

Sadness is related to the heart chakra and indicates unresolved issues regarding love and forgiveness. It also points to the solar plexus chakra, associated with personal power and self-confidence, as sadness results from challenges in expressing your true essence.

Stress:

Stress is a common emotion in busy life, but it also indicates that you are overwhelmed or out of alignment in your needs and limits. Prolonged stress leads to energy blockages in different areas. It is related to the solar plexus chakra, indicating emotional overload and misalignment with one's limits and needs.

Anxiety:

Anxiety suggests that you are worried about the future or stuck in negative mental patterns. It indicates an imbalance in the laryngeal chakra related to communication and self-expression. Feeling anxious indicates worries about the future or difficulty expressing your needs and emotions clearly.

Anger:

Anger is an indicator that you are repressing emotions or facing challenging situations. It points to blockages in the solar plexus chakra, which is related to personal power and self-confidence. Anger triggers imbalances in personal power and self-control, indicating unresolved issues regarding forgiveness and compassion.

Fear:

Fear reveals that you are feeling insecure or threatened in some area of life. It indicates blockages in the root chakra, which is associated with security and stability. Feeling afraid indicates insecurity or threat in some area of life.

Guilt:

Feeling guilt suggests that you are over-charging yourself or that you are carrying emotional burdens from the past. Guilt is related to blockages in the heart chakra, which is associated with love and forgiveness, indicating unresolved issues. It is also linked to the solar plexus chakra, indicating excessive self-blaming and a lack of self-esteem.

This approach considers that different emotions can be related to different chakras, since emotional experiences are complex and multifaceted. It's important to remember that the connection between emotions and chakras can vary depending on the person, so continuous self-observation and honesty about your own feelings are fundamental to identifying how your emotions relate to your chakras and your general energy.

Practicing mindfulness is also a powerful way of developing energetic awareness. By being fully aware of the present moment, you become aware of how different situations, people or environments affect your energy and well-being.

Your body is a valuable source of information about your internal energy. Notice if you feel any tension, pain or discomfort anywhere. These physical symptoms are reflections of energy blockages or imbalances.

Keep a journal or notebook to record your observations and insights throughout the day. Write down how you feel, what emotions arise in different situations and what energetic patterns you notice. This practice helps to consolidate energetic awareness and identify recurring patterns.

Ask yourself about your emotions and energy. For example: "Why am I feeling this way?" or "What is causing this blockage?" Talk to yourself sincerely and receptively, seeking to understand your inner energies more deeply.

When you identify blockages or imbalances, look for ways to bring harmony and balance to your energy. This can include meditation practices, conscious breathing, visualizations, physical exercises, energy therapies or any other techniques that resonate with you.

Remember that energy awareness is an ongoing process and requires practice and patience. The more you connect with your inner energy and observe your emotions and thoughts, the easier it becomes to identify blockages and imbalances in your daily life. This practice not only enables self-knowledge, but also offers opportunities for personal and spiritual growth, promoting greater well-being and harmony in life.

Once you are aware of your energies, it's time to dedicate precious time to energy alignment practices. Set aside a quiet moment in your routine to connect with your inner essence and work on balancing your chakras, realigning your energy in a harmonious way. The techniques you've learned throughout the book, such as meditation, visualization and conscious breathing, will be your allies on this journey.

During your meditation sessions, allow yourself to dive deep into your being, exploring each chakra and its specific energies. Visualize the purifying light enveloping you, releasing blockages and allowing energy to flow freely. Focus on each chakra, from the root to the crown, and feel the energy aligning and expanding throughout the body.

As you practice visualization, imagine yourself surrounded by a bright, welcoming light, nourishing and strengthening your energy field. See your aura glowing with intensity, reflecting the balance and harmony you are cultivating internally.

Conscious breathing is another powerful tool for aligning your energies. Take a few minutes to breathe deeply, bringing your attention to your breath, allowing it to calm your mind and soothe your emotions. As you breathe in, imagine that you are absorbing vital energy and light. As you exhale, release any accumulated tension or negative energy.

These energy alignment practices will not only strengthen your energy field, but also increase your intuition and spiritual awareness. You will feel more connected with yourself and the world around you, finding deep balance in all aspects of life.

In addition to energy alignment practices, it's important to know that nutrition plays a crucial role in integrating this alignment into your lifestyle. Pay attention to the fact that everything you consume, whether in terms of food, thoughts or external influences, has a direct impact on your energy. Therefore, make conscious choices when selecting foods, opting for those that are fresh, vibrant and nutritious, capable of providing the body with vital energy.

Prioritize a diet rich in nutrients that support your physical and energetic health. Eat fruits and vegetables that are colorful and varied, as each color represents different benefits for the body and mind. A balanced and healthy diet provides you with the energy you need to feel strong and invigorated.

As well as nourishing your body physically, pay attention to the thoughts and emotions you nurture on a daily basis. Cultivate a positive and loving mindset, try to direct your attention to constructive and uplifting thoughts. By doing this, you create an internal environment conducive to energy alignment, allowing your energy to flow harmoniously.

Be kind to yourself and others, and try to stay away from negative or self-critical thoughts. Instead, find ways to nurture self-love and self-acceptance, as these feelings strengthen your connection to positive energy.

The journey of energetic alignment is unique to each individual and is a continuous process of learning and growth. As you become more aware of your food choices, thoughts and emotions, you build a solid foundation for a positive energetic lifestyle, promoting greater well-being in all aspects of life.

Another fundamental aspect of integrating energetic alignment into your life is to create a physical and energetic environment conducive to spiritual growth. Take the time to organize and clean your space, ensuring that it is free of clutter and stagnant energies. Harmony in your environment reflects directly on your inner energy, promoting greater balance and well-being.

Start by organizing your belongings and getting rid of unnecessary items. Get rid of objects that no longer bring you joy or usefulness, as they accumulate stagnant energy and hinder the energetic flow in your space. By creating an organized and clutter-free environment, you allow energy to flow freely, favoring energetic alignment.

In addition to organization, use energy cleansing techniques to purify the environment. Smoking with sacred herbs, such as sage or palo santo, is an effective ancient practice for removing negative energies and revitalizing the space. By lighting the incense of one of these elements and spreading the smoke to every corner of your home, you will be releasing stagnant energies, bringing a sense of renewal and clarity. Use the following sacred herbs for energy cleansing:

White Sage:

White sage is an herb widely used for energy cleansing. Light an incense stick of white sage and allow the purifying smoke to spread around the room, passing through corners and spaces where energy may be stagnant. While doing this, focus on the intention of releasing any negative energy to promote harmony in your space.

Rosemary:

Rosemary is known for its cleansing and protective properties. Burn some rosemary leaves or incense and allow the smoke to spread around the room. As you do so, visualize negative energy being dissolved and replaced by positive, revitalizing energy.

Lavender:

Lavender is a sacred herb associated with peace, relaxation and balance. Use lavender essential oil to create an energy cleansing spray. Mix a few drops of lavender essential oil in distilled water and spray it in your environment, visualizing the energy being purified and harmonized.

Basil:

Basil is a sacred herb that helps cleanse and protect space. Put some fresh basil leaves in a container and leave it in your room. As well as releasing a pleasant aroma, basil also drives away negative energies, promoting an atmosphere of tranquillity.

Another way to raise the vibration of your environment is to use crystals at strategic points. Choose crystals that resonate with your intentions and spiritual goals, such as clear quartz for purification, amethyst for harmony and protection, or citrine to attract prosperity and abundance. Place these crystals in places where their frequency is highest, such as your work desk, bedroom or meditation area.

By taking the time and care to create a healthy physical and energetic environment, you provide a welcoming space for spiritual growth. This helps you feel more connected with yourself and the energies of the universe, expanding your capacity for energetic alignment and promoting a meaningful and enriching spiritual journey. Remember that every little adjustment to your environment makes a big difference to your energy and general well-being.

Although the properties of the main crystals are listed on previous pages, here are some of the crystals you can insert into your environment to boost your energy and harmony.

White Quartz:

White quartz is known for its ability to purify and clarify energy. Place a white quartz crystal in a central location in your space to amplify positive energy and neutralize negative influences.

Amethyst:

Amethyst is a powerful crystal that raises the spiritual vibration, promoting calm and inner peace. Place a pile of amethysts in your environment to create an atmosphere of tranquillity and spiritual connection.

Citrine:

Citrine is associated with joy, prosperity and positive energy. Place a few citrine crystals in strategic areas of your space to attract abundance and vitality.

Selenite:

Selenite is a crystal that promotes energy cleansing and mental clarity. Place one or more slabs of selenite in your environment to help remove negative energies and stimulate harmony and balance.

Sodium Crystal (Salt Stone)

Sodium crystal, also known as salt stone, is a natural crystal that is easily found. Place small portions of salt stone in a significant place in your space to purify the energy and bring a sense of cleanliness and balance. Salt stone has the property of absorbing negative energies from the environment, promoting an atmosphere of renewal and well-being.

Integrating energy alignment with your lifestyle also extends to the way you relate to others and the community. Seek to nurture healthy, balanced relationships based on respect, compassion and mutual support. Value meaningful connections with people who share similar spiritual interests, and where you can find support and encouragement.

Participating in groups or communities with spiritual affinities is a valuable opportunity to enrich your spiritual journey. By joining with others who are seeking spiritual growth and upliftment, you have the chance to share experiences, learnings and practices, enriching your own understanding and advancing along the path of energetic alignment.

Collaborating and exchanging energies with others in a supportive and understanding space strengthens spiritual convictions and broadens horizons. Sharing and receiving knowledge with empathy and openness creates an atmosphere of collective growth, in which everyone is nourished by the experiences and insights of others.

It is important to realize that integrating energy alignment is not an isolated practice, but a holistic approach to living in harmony with the universe. By bringing this awareness and practice into your daily life, you open up space for spiritual growth and deepen your connection with your inner self.

This continuous search for a more harmonious and meaningful life leads to a deep connection with yourself, allowing your spiritual potential to flourish. The process is transformative and provides growth, well-being and a greater sense of purpose in life's journey.

In this process, remember to be kind. The spiritual journey is unique, and it is normal to face challenges and moments of reflection along the way. Allow yourself to grow at your own pace, honoring your needs and intuitions.

27
Conscious Manifestation

Learn about the principles of conscious manifestation in Cosmic Spirituality. This is the process where you intentionally create the reality you desire, using energy, intention and consciousness as powerful tools. The Beings of Light have a deep understanding of these principles and offer this valuable knowledge on how you can become a conscious co-creator of your reality.

Although this topic has been covered on previous pages, let's delve a little deeper.

In Cosmic Spirituality, your thoughts and intentions have undeniable power in creating reality. Everything that exists in the universe is energy, and your thoughts and intentions are forms of energy that you send into the quantum field of universal consciousness. Therefore, in order to manifest consciously, it is essential to cultivate a heightened awareness and direct your thoughts and intentions towards what you want to create. By focusing your energy positively and in line with your values and purposes, you begin to attract experiences and circumstances that are in tune with your intentions.

One of the fundamental principles of conscious manifestation is vibrational alignment. This means that in order to manifest your desires, you must vibrate at the same energetic frequency as what you want to attract. When you are in vibrational harmony with your desires, you create a resonance field that allows these desires and experiences to manifest in your life. Therefore, it is important to cultivate positive emotions, such as gratitude, joy and love, to release any energetic blockages that may prevent your vibrational alignment. Practices such as meditation, visualization and positive affirmations are useful in this alignment process.

In Cosmic Spirituality you are part of an interconnected and intelligent universe. Conscious manifestation is not just an individual act, but a co-creation with the Universe. By establishing a partnership with the cosmos, you open up space to receive guidance, synchronicities and opportunities that help you manifest your desires in a fluid and harmonious way. This requires trust in the wisdom of the Universe and a willingness to act in alignment with the signs and directions you receive. By co-creating with the Universe, you recognize that your desires and intentions can manifest in even more surprising ways than you can imagine.

While it is important to set clear intentions and visualize what you want to manifest, it is also essential to practice detachment and trust in the process. Excessive attachment to the outcome creates resistance and limits the flow of energy. Trust allows you to open up to possibilities beyond your current understanding, allowing the Universe to manifest in ways that may surprise you. Trusting and surrendering to the flow of the Universe is an essential aspect of conscious manifestation in Cosmic Spirituality.

Conscious manifestation is not only based on thoughts and intentions, but also requires inspired and intuitive action. As you align with your intentions and receive guidance from the Universe, you are called to act in a way that is congruent with these intentions. This action is subtle and based on intuition, leading you to opportunities and synchronicities that bring you closer to your desires. It is important to cultivate the awareness and receptivity to recognize these opportunities and to have the courage to act when intuition indicates the best path.

In Cosmic Spirituality, conscious manifestation is seen as a natural ability, an expression of your power as a spiritual being. By understanding and applying the principles of conscious manifestation, you transform your life and co-create a reality aligned with your highest essence. Remember that conscious manifestation requires practice, patience and perseverance. As you delve deeper into this process, you become more aware of your ability to create and manifest your dreams.

28
Creative Visualization

The practice of creative visualization is the power to focus on your desired reality. Creative visualization is a powerful tool that allows you to direct your imagination and energy towards manifesting your deepest desires. The Beings of Light know the transformative potential of this practice and offer valuable guidance on how to use it to create the desired reality.

Creative visualization is the ability to form vivid and detailed mental images that represent your desired reality. When you visualize with clarity and intensity, you are activating the same brain centers that would be activated if you were experiencing that situation in real time. This practice stimulates the subconscious mind, which is responsible for influencing your beliefs, emotions and behavior. By repeatedly visualizing a desired reality, you reprogram the subconscious mind to manifest that reality in conscious experience.

To use creative visualization effectively, it's important to cultivate clarity about what you want to manifest. Setting clear and specific goals helps you direct your energy and attention towards the desired manifestation. The more detailed the visualizations, the more powerful they become. When visualizing, you can include not only images, but also sensations, emotions and even internal dialogues that are aligned with the desired reality. In this way, you create a complete, immersive experience in the mind, enabling this experience to manifest itself in your external reality.

Creative visualization requires focus and persistence. It's important to set aside time each day to practice it, creating a peaceful and supportive environment. By committing yourself and devoting time and energy to visualization, you demonstrate intention and commitment to the manifestation of your desires. The more consistent you are, the quicker you will see results. Although it's normal for doubts or obstacles to arise along the way, it's essential to stay focused on your desired reality.

As explained earlier, the cosmic energies capable of bringing what you desire from the energetic world to the physical world are intrinsically linked to love, so one way of aligning your desire with this concept is to project it towards common well-being.

By creating the mental image associated with the common good, your subconscious awakens to the basic principle of spirituality, love, promoting a change in your mental state, aligning your energy with the energy of the source that creates everything, out of love.

Just to make this more understandable, let's assume that the desired materialization is an improvement in your financial situation. In this case, visualize how you can contribute to the common good when this reality materializes. For example, imagine yourself donating to charities, buying medicine for those who need it, financing medical treatment for those who can't afford it or donating food to those who are hungry. This may seem like a selfish way of achieving the goal, but this visualization aligns your desire to materialize with the basic principle of solidarity, and this changes your mental pattern. Thinking that this kind of thinking is selfish means that you are stuck in pre-established patterns. Unfortunately, 99% of people have been taught that the rich will not inherit the Kingdom of Heaven, so their subconscious fights against ways of achieving higher standards of consciousness. You have to overcome these ties, after all, what would become of the planet if everyone was poor?

In this way, by manifesting your desires connected to generosity and caring for others, contributing to a more loving and harmonious world, you open up the connection with the energy that creates everything.

A fundamental part of creative visualization is the incorporation of positive emotions associated with the desired reality. When visualizing, you must allow yourself to feel the emotions of joy, gratitude and satisfaction that you will experience when you experience that reality. Emotions are a powerful form of energy and act like magnets that attract similar experiences. The more intensely you feel these positive emotions during visualization, the more quickly you will be aligned with the desired reality and the more ready you will be for it to manifest.

When practicing creative visualization and focusing on the desired reality, it is important to cultivate trust and surrender to the Universe. Know that there is a greater cosmic intelligence at play and that you are co-creating with this intelligence. You must trust that the Universe is always supporting you and working in your favor, even if the results don't immediately manifest in the way you expect. Surrender allows unexpected solutions and higher paths to reveal themselves, making room for a manifestation beyond your expectations.

Creative visualization and focusing on the desired reality are powerful practices in Cosmic Spirituality. Through them, you can direct your imagination and energy towards manifesting your deepest desires. By practicing creative visualization with clarity, focus, persistence and positive emotions, you align your mind and heart with the reality you want to create. With trust and surrender to the Universe, you allow the process of manifestation to unfold in magical and surprising ways.

29
Empowering Manifestation

Cosmic energy is a high frequency that has a direct connection with cosmic consciousness and its advanced technologies. This energy is a powerful ally for the conscious manifestation of desires. By aligning with Cosmic energy, you can amplify and accelerate the manifestation process, bringing what you desire into your reality.

To enhance manifestation with Cosmic energy, it is important to establish a conscious connection with this energy. You can do this through meditation, visualization or other spiritual practices already mentioned in this book. By tuning in to Cosmic energy, you open up a channel of communication and collaboration with the Beings of Light, knowing that they are ready to assist your manifestation journey.

The Cosmic frequency is a frequency of love, wisdom and creative power. To enhance manifestation, it is important to raise your vibration and align yourself with this frequency. You can achieve this by cultivating positive thoughts, practicing gratitude, taking care of your physical and emotional well-being, and maintaining a clear intention focused on your desires. The more you tune in to the Cosmic frequency, the more harmonized you are with the flow of manifestation.

Perhaps it's not very explanatory to talk about frequency without explaining the difference between this frequency and the common knowledge meaning of the term.

In didactic terms, "Cosmic Frequency" refers to a specific level or pattern of energy, or vibration associated with concepts of love, wisdom and creative power. In this spiritual context, frequency is not a measure of repetitive cycles per unit of time, as we normally understand it in physical terms. Instead, it is a metaphorical reference that describes the energetic and emotional state you are in.

Imagine that every emotion, thought and intention has a "vibration" or energetic quality. For example, feelings of love and gratitude have a high, positive vibration, while feelings of anger and sadness have a lower, denser vibration. The Cosmic frequency represents a high state of energy, in which feelings of love, wisdom and creative power predominate.

The difference between this sense of frequency and physical frequency is that Cosmic frequency is not related to a measure of time or waves as we normally associate it with. Instead, it is a way of describing a person's emotional and energetic state, emphasizing the importance of cultivating positive thoughts and feelings to align with this higher frequency.

To enhance manifestation, i.e. to make your desires and intentions a reality, it is suggested that you tune in to the Cosmic frequency, raising your vibration to a more positive and harmonious state. This is achieved by practicing positive thoughts, being grateful for the good things in life, taking care of your physical and emotional well-being, and focusing clearly on your desires and goals.

The more you align and tune in to the Cosmic frequency, the more you are in harmony with the flow of manifestation, making it likely that your intentions and desires will come true. This spiritual approach emphasizes the power of energy and emotions in your life, and how you can direct them to create a more positive reality aligned with your goals.

The Beings of Light are known for having access to the forces that facilitate manifestation and healing. You can connect with these beings energetically and imaginatively, and you can also visualize these forces in light forms, using them to amplify your manifestation processes. This practice strengthens your connection with Cosmic energy and enhances your manifesting power.

To visualize Cosmic energy and connect with the Beings of Light, you can imagine yourself in a special healing chamber. Close your eyes and take a few deep breaths to relax and concentrate. Visualize yourself in a space surrounded by bright white light, which represents high-vibration Cosmic energy.

In this Cosmic healing chamber, feel yourself enveloped by a loving and powerful energy, capable of accelerating the manifestation of your desires. Feel this energy penetrating every cell of your body, bringing a sense of balance, harmony and healing.

Imagine that this cosmic energy is attuned to your deepest desires and clear intentions. Visualize your goals and dreams materializing in front of you, as if they were being brought to reality by a light, easily and quickly.

Feel connected to the wisdom and creative power of Cosmic energy, allowing it to amplify your manifestation processes. Feel safe and confident in this energetic space, knowing that you have access to the forces that create your desired reality.

As you connect with Cosmic energy, notice how your manifesting power is enhanced. Feel empowered to bring out your most authentic desires and manifest them in an aligned and harmonious way.

Hold this mental image for as long as you wish, absorbing the Cosmic energy and feeling strengthened by this energetic connection. When you open your eyes, take with you the feeling of empowerment and confidence, knowing that you have the capacity to manifest your dreams with the support of Cosmic energy.

A clear intention is fundamental to conscious manifestation. You must be clear about what you want to manifest and keep your intention firm and focused on that goal. By working with Cosmic energy, you can strengthen your intention, allowing it to be driven by the high-frequency energy of the Beings of Light. It is important to remember that the intention must be aligned with the greater good of everyone involved.

One of the many ways to achieve the state of conscious manifestation is to create a mental image of what you want to manifest after a moment of meditation (already explained on previous pages). While holding this image, open yourself up to the cosmic energy available. Imagine a stream of brilliant white light coming from space, bringing with it wisdom and manifesting power. This energy surrounds you, filling you with a sense of strength and determination.

Remember that when you manifest your desires, they can impact the whole, so always seek the common benefit.

Stay in the present moment, trusting in the flow of cosmic energy that works in tune with your intention.

Believe in your ability to co-create your reality and know that, with clarity, focus and alignment, you are on the right path and your dreams will manifest consciously.

Practice this energetic connection, with clear intention, regularly allowing the Cosmic energy to strengthen the manifesting process. As you become more aware of this powerful collaboration between your intention and Cosmic energy, you are cultivating a meaningful relationship with conscious manifestation.

The Beings of Light are ready to assist your manifestation journey. You can invite them to be your co-creation partners by sharing your desires and goals and requesting their assistance. You can ask for guidance, clarity and signs to help you follow the path of manifestation. By opening up this communication and trusting in the wisdom and support of the Beings of Light, you enhance the manifestation process that allows creative and harmonious solutions to manifest in your reality.

Empowering manifestation with Cosmic energy is an opportunity to accelerate the process of conscious creation. By connecting to Cosmic energy, you raise your vibration, aligning yourself with a frequency of love, wisdom and creative power. Using Cosmic technologies, you strengthen your intention and clarity, co-creating with the Beings of Light in the quest to materialize your highest desires. By integrating this approach into your daily practice, you experience a faster, more fluid manifestation that is aligned with your true essence.

30
Aligned Co-creation

Co-creation, as mentioned earlier, is a powerful process in which you join with the Universe to manifest your desires, creating a reality aligned with your purpose. This involves exploring who you are, your values, passions and unique gifts. When you are aligned with your purpose, your desires for manifestation are a natural extension of the connection. By tuning in to your purpose, you open up space for co-creation to take place in an authentic and meaningful way.

Clarity about your desires is a fundamental aspect of co-creation. This involves identifying what you really want to manifest. The idea of manifestation usually leads us to imagine something tangible, concrete. However, it is essential to remember that you may wish to manifest greater spiritual clarity, well-being for yourself or others, and even the manifestation of happiness.

It's important to direct your desires within the realm of possibility, not because there are limitations to what you can wish to manifest, but to avoid frustration. For example, wishing for an elephant to flap its wings may be unattainable in reality. By being specific and detailed when describing your wishes, you facilitate communication with the Universe. Clarity in your desires directs your energy and intention towards what really matters, allowing co-creation to take place more effectively, in line with the Universal Flow.

Harmonizing with the Universal Flow involves being in connection with the natural flow of energy and information that permeates the universe. It's like sailing on a river of possibilities and synchronicities. To better understand the concept of Universal Flow, think of the analogy of a current: when you align yourself with it, you are carried smoothly in the same direction as the flow of water, effortlessly.

Imagine yourself as part of a vast interconnected system, in which everything is in constant movement and interaction. In this system, there is a greater intelligence, a divine order that guides and coordinates all events and circumstances. This cosmic order is the Universal Flow, the current.

Being in harmony with the Universal Flow means being in tune with the greater intelligence, trusting that everything happens at the right time and in the right way. This doesn't mean that you don't have free will, but rather that your choices are guided by a greater wisdom that is in harmony with the whole.

To align with the Universal Flow, it's important to cultivate awareness of the present moment. Be open and receptive to what is happening in your life, paying attention to the opportunities and signals that the universe sends you. This requires being present and aware, letting go of past worries or future anxieties.

Another fundamental aspect is to trust yourself and your intuitions. Sometimes the Universal Flow can seem challenging or take you down unexpected paths, but trust that everything is contributing to your growth and learning. Believe in your ability to deal with the situations that arise and make decisions in line with your purposes and values.

Co-creation in harmony with the Universal Flow is more than just manifesting your personal desires; it's about creating a meaningful life that is aligned with the whole. This requires the humility to recognize that you are part of something bigger and that your journey is connected to other people, the planet and the physical and extraphysical universe.

Practice gratitude and acceptance, recognizing that everything that happens in your life is part of a bigger plan. By living in harmony with the Universal Flow, you experience fluidity, purpose and well-being, you become a conscious co-creator of your own reality.

Trust is a key element in co-creation. You must trust the process and the power of the Universe to guide and manifest your desires. This involves letting go of the need for control and being willing to surrender to the flow of life, to the current. When you trust and surrender, you open up space for co-creation to unfold in magical and surprising ways.

Although co-creation involves trusting in the power of the Universe, it is also important to take inspired actions towards your desires. These actions are guided by intuition and are aligned with a purpose. By acting in an inspired way, you demonstrate your commitment and desire to co-create your reality. Remember that co-creation is a collaboration between you and the Universe, and both parties play an active role in this process.

Gratitude is fundamental to co-creation. When you express gratitude for what you already have and for the manifestations that are on their way, you are tuning your vibration to the power of love and appreciation. Gratitude also strengthens your connection with the Universe and puts you in a state of receiving, allowing co-creation to flow harmoniously and abundantly.

Co-creation aligned with purpose and harmony is a powerful way of manifesting desires and creating a meaningful reality. By connecting to your purpose, you clarify your desires. Being in harmony with the universal flow, you trust and surrender, take inspired action and express gratitude, making space for co-creation to flow in your life.

31
Levels of Consciousness

Cosmic Spirituality is an approach that recognizes the existence of multiple levels of consciousness and the importance of exploring them on the spiritual journey. It is important to advance in your understanding in order to identify how these levels of consciousness relate to your life experience.

The most basic level of consciousness is everyday consciousness, which is focused on everyday tasks and challenges. In this state, you are mainly concerned with your physical needs, emotions and social interactions. Although this level of consciousness is necessary for dealing with the practical demands of life, it tends to be limited and superficial.

Beyond everyday awareness, there is the level of self-conscious awareness, where you begin to question your identity and deeper purpose. At this stage, you become aware of yourself as a unique being who seeks to understand your relationship with the world around you. Self-reflection and self-knowledge are key aspects of this level of consciousness.

On the other hand, expanded consciousness is a higher level in which you begin to transcend your individual identity, connecting to a broader, more universal consciousness. In this state, you experience a sense of unity with all that exists, recognizing that you are part of an interconnected whole. Practices such as meditation, contemplation and altered states of consciousness help you access and explore this expanded level.

At the highest level of consciousness, known as cosmic consciousness, you are able to connect with the wisdom and intelligence of the universe. There are many names for this wisdom, some religions call it God. In this state, you experience a profound understanding of nature and reality, transcending the limits of time and space. It is at this level that you access information and insights beyond rational comprehension, with a clearer vision of your spiritual purpose.

In Cosmic Spirituality, consciousness is a state that aligns with the principles and teachings transmitted by the Beings of Light. This consciousness emphasizes compassion, healing, cosmic wisdom and service to others. It is a state of consciousness that connects you with the energy and vibrational frequency of the Beings of Light, allowing you to receive guidance and support on your spiritual journey.

Exploring the different levels of consciousness in Cosmic Spirituality offers the opportunity for growth, expansion and alignment with your true spiritual nature. As you delve deeper into this exploration, you experience greater clarity, inner peace and connection with something greater than yourself.

32
Expansion of Consciousness

The expansion of consciousness is a central theme in Cosmic Spirituality, which recognizes the importance of raising consciousness in order to achieve a deep understanding of yourself, others and the world around you. It is therefore important to explore the expansion of consciousness in depth, both on an individual and collective level, highlighting its importance and benefits in the spiritual journey for the evolution of humanity as a whole.

The expansion of individual consciousness refers to the process of raising perception and understanding beyond the limits of everyday consciousness. It involves seeking self-knowledge, exploring beliefs and thought patterns and opening up to new perspectives and possibilities. By expanding individual consciousness, you experience a greater sense of purpose, a connection with your spiritual essence and a broader view of life.

Expanding individual consciousness is a fascinating and transformative path that allows you to explore the depths of your being and connect with the vastness of the universe. One of the most powerful ways to embark on this journey is through the regular practice of meditation. Meditation is a technique that leads to a state of mental stillness, allowing you to transcend thoughts by immersing yourself in a space of pure presence.

During meditation, you become an attentive observer of your mind, observing feelings and physical sensations, without judgment or attachment. By calming mental agitation, you open up space for greater intuitive perception, accessing the inner wisdom that is often obscured amid the noise of everyday life. This practice not only expands individual awareness, but is also beneficial for mental and emotional health, reducing stress and increasing mental clarity.

In addition to meditation, exploring different spiritual traditions and studying philosophies are also valuable tools for expanding consciousness. Each spiritual tradition offers unique perspectives on life, purpose and the connection with the divine. By immersing yourself in different spiritual teachings, you can find inspiration, deep understanding and answers to your own existential questions.

However, it's important to remember that the expansion of consciousness is an ongoing and personal process. Each person has their own rhythm. It is essential to be open and receptive, allowing your consciousness to expand naturally. Regular meditation practice and exploring different spiritual traditions and philosophies are just some of the possible paths to this growth.

By expanding your individual consciousness, you open up to new perspectives and deeper understandings, establishing a more intimate connection with the universe and with yourself. This journey of expansion is enriching and transformative, leading you to a more conscious, empathetic and connected state with the greatness of existence.

As well as individual consciousness, collective consciousness can also be expanded. Collective consciousness refers to the energy and awareness shared by a group of individuals or even humanity as a whole. When many individuals come together with a common goal, they raise their consciousness by creating a powerful synergy that positively affects everyone's consciousness.

The expansion of collective consciousness involves creating a greater awareness of unity, compassion and cooperation. It is the recognition that everyone is interconnected and that our actions and thoughts have an impact beyond ourselves. Raising collective consciousness promotes healing, transformation and spiritual awakening on a global scale.

The practice of group meditation, rituals of spiritual connection and participation in conscious communities are some of the ways in which you contribute to the expansion of collective consciousness. In addition, the dissemination of knowledge, positive values and compassionate attitudes play a fundamental role in the transformation of collective consciousness.

The expansion of consciousness, both individual and collective, brings numerous benefits to the spiritual journey and to the evolution of humanity as a whole. Some of these benefits include:

Greater clarity and understanding about your true spiritual essence;

Development of a broader vision of life and personal purpose;

Deepening interpersonal connections and more meaningful relationships;

A sense of inner peace and harmony;

Ability to cope better with challenges and adversity;

Greater empathy and compassion for others;

Contribution to the creation of a more conscious and harmonious world.

The expansion of individual and collective consciousness does not happen overnight. It is a continuous process of growth, learning and self-discovery. It requires dedication, practice and openness to explore beyond the limits of conventional consciousness. As you commit to this journey of expanding consciousness, you not only enrich your own life, but also contribute to the evolution of humanity as a whole.

The expansion of consciousness allows access to higher states of perception, understanding of your true spiritual essence, contributing to the evolution of humanity. This book is an invitation for you to continue your journey of expanding your consciousness by sharing the benefits of this experience with the world around you.

33
Higher Dimensions and Beings of Light

Cosmic Spirituality speaks of the existence of higher dimensions inhabited by Beings of Light, so let's explore the importance and benefits of connecting with these dimensions and learn about practices that will help you on this journey.

According to Cosmic Spirituality, the universe is made up of many other dimensions besides the physical one in which you live. These higher dimensions are realms of higher consciousness, where the energy is more subtle and the laws of reality are different from those experienced on your earthly plane.

Connecting to the higher dimensions means opening yourself up to the possibility of interacting with Beings of Light, spirit guides and the other forms of consciousness that reside in these dimensions. This connection brings insights, spiritual guidance and a greater sense of purpose on the journey.

The Beings of Light are spiritual entities who inhabit the higher dimensions and are characterized by wisdom, unconditional love and a desire to help humanity grow spiritually. These beings present themselves in different forms, such as angels, archangels, ascended masters or spiritual guides.

Connecting with the Beings of Light is a source of inspiration, healing and support on the spiritual journey. They offer guidance, protection and assistance in spiritual practices. By establishing a conscious relationship with these beings, you open doors to receiving messages, wisdom and loving energy.

There are various practices that help you connect with the higher dimensions and the Beings of Light, meditation being one of them. By dedicating regular time to meditation, you strengthen your spiritual connection, opening doors to communication with Beings of Light.

Through creative visualization you can create a sacred space in your mind and invite Beings of Light to assist you on your journey. You can imagine yourself in a peaceful and safe place, and then set a clear intention to connect with Beings of Light to receive guidance.

Developing intuition and energetic perception helps you recognize the presence of Beings of Light and receive their messages. By practicing inner listening and tuning in to the subtle energies around you, you become more receptive to the guidance you receive.

Performing rituals and sacred ceremonies creates a space conducive to connecting with higher dimensions. You can create an altar, light candles, burn incense or make prayers and invocations to invite the Beings of Light to accompany you during these special moments.

By developing a conscious connection with the higher dimensions and the Beings of Light, you experience a number of benefits. The Beings of Light offer guidance, insights and spiritual wisdom to help you on your evolutionary journey.

Connecting with Beings of Light facilitates emotional, mental and spiritual healing processes, releasing limiting patterns so that you reach a state of balance and wholeness.

Beings of Light radiate unconditional love, and by connecting with them, you experience this deep and transformative love in your life.

Connecting with higher dimensions and Beings of Light helps you discover how to live according to your highest purpose, providing direction and clarity regarding the path to follow.

Connecting with higher dimensions and Beings of Light is an essential part of Cosmic Spirituality. By opening up to these subtle dimensions, establishing a conscious relationship with the Beings of Light, you receive spiritual guidance, healing and transformation on your personal journey. This book invites you to explore these practices by developing your own connection with the higher dimensions and the Beings of Light, allowing your life to be guided by the wisdom and love of the higher dimensions.

34
Spiritual DNA

The Awakening of Cosmic Consciousness

Cosmic Spirituality knows the human potential for the activation of spiritual DNA and the awakening of cosmic consciousness. In this process you can engage in practices that stimulate this activation for the expansion of consciousness.

According to Cosmic Spirituality, spiritual DNA is an aspect of our genetic code that contains information of a spiritual and multidimensional nature. This DNA is made up of strands in addition to the two physical strands that conventional science recognizes.

Throughout the ages, humanity's spiritual DNA has been largely dormant, limiting our perception of reality and our potential as spiritual beings. However, with the evolution of human consciousness comes the possibility of reactivating these filaments, allowing us to access expanded states of consciousness and experience reality in a broad and profound way.

As explained above, the awakening of cosmic consciousness refers to the expansion of perception beyond the limits of the individual self and physical reality. It is the ability to connect and recognize the interconnection with the Universe, understanding oneself as part of a vast web of energy and consciousness.

This awakening allows you to access information and wisdom that goes beyond conventional knowledge, opening up communication with Beings of Light, spiritual guides and cosmic intelligences, allowing you to experience states of unity, unconditional love and expanded consciousness.

There are various practices that help in the process of activating spiritual DNA and awakening cosmic consciousness.

Meditation is a powerful tool that calms the mind and opens up the connection with your spiritual essence. Through the practice of meditation, you access states of expanded consciousness, allowing energy to flow freely and stimulating the activation of spiritual DNA.

Creative visualization can also be used to connect you with images and symbols that represent your connection with the cosmos.

Spending time in nature is also an effective way of connecting with the natural flow of life and tuning into cosmic energies. Walking in the forest, meditating outdoors or simply being in contact with the beauty of nature will remind you of your connection with the universe, awakening the cosmic consciousness within you.

Sounds, mantras and music with specific frequencies are used to stimulate and awaken the energy of spiritual DNA. Sacred sounds, such as OM, create resonance in your system, activating dormant parts of the spiritual DNA.

The awakening of cosmic consciousness brings a number of benefits to your life and spiritual evolution. Some of these benefits include:

Expansion of perception:

As you awaken to cosmic consciousness, your perception expands beyond the limits of the individual self, allowing you to interconnect with all things and to understand the multidimensional nature of reality.

As you open up to cosmic consciousness, you have access to information and wisdom that goes beyond conventional knowledge. This allows you to make decisions more in line with your purpose by receiving guidance from higher sources.

The awakening of cosmic consciousness connects you with the essence of unconditional love, allowing you to experience and share this love more fully and compassionately.

By expanding cosmic consciousness, you also increase your ability to intentionally manifest your desires, creating the reality aligned with your highest purpose.

The activation of spiritual DNA and the awakening of cosmic consciousness are fundamental processes. By opening up to the higher dimensions of your existence, you expand your perception, access higher wisdom and guidance, experience unconditional love and consciously manifest your desired reality.

35
Integrating the Expansion of Consciousness

The expansion of consciousness (as discussed on previous pages) is a fundamental aspect of the spiritual journey. As you open up to higher levels of perception and understanding, you become able to experience reality in a deeper and more meaningful way.

Expanding consciousness involves broadening your perception and understanding of reality. As you move beyond the limits of ordinary consciousness, you become able to access information, insights and experiences that are beyond the comprehension of your limited self.

This expansion occurs through spiritual practices, meditation, connection with nature, transformative encounters or experiences of transcendence. As your consciousness expands, you begin to experience a greater connection with the divine, a sense of unity with the whole and a deeper understanding of your purpose and meaning in life.

Although the expansion of consciousness is a powerful experience, it is equally important to integrate this expansion into everyday life. Integration involves bringing insights, learnings and experiences from the expansion of consciousness into everyday life, allowing them to transform your actions, choices and interactions.

Without proper integration, the expansion of consciousness becomes an isolated experience, disconnected from reality. True transformation occurs when you integrate these new perspectives into your way of being and living, incorporating them into your relationships, work, spiritual practices and lifestyle.

There are various practices that help you integrate the expansion of consciousness into your spiritual journey.

Take time regularly to reflect on your consciousness-expanding experiences. Ask yourself how these experiences can be applied in your life. Consider what insights and learnings you can bring to your interactions, choices and spiritual practices.

Use anchoring practices to bring the expansion of consciousness into the physical body and the present moment. Examples include rootedness meditation, conscious breathing exercises, nature walks or any activity that helps you connect with the body and the here and now.

Many of the options mentioned in the previous paragraph have been covered on previous pages, but I think it's important to go into more detail about anchoring and rootedness, so that your understanding of the subject is complete.

Anchoring is a practice that aims to bring the expansion of consciousness into the physical body and the present moment. It's a way of connecting with reality here and now.

To perform anchoring, you can follow these steps:

Find a quiet, comfortable place to sit or stand.

Close your eyes and take a few deep breaths to relax and calm your mind.

Focus your attention on your breathing, observing how the air flows in and out.

Then bring your attention to the points of contact between your body and the floor or surface you are standing on. Feel the sensation of support and stability that contact with the ground provides.

As you focus on the points of contact, visualize roots coming out of your body and extending to the Earth's core.

Stay with this feeling of connection for a few minutes, feeling anchored to the present moment.

Anchoring is a simple and powerful technique that can be practiced daily to find calm, balance and presence in the midst of everyday hustle and bustle.

Rooting, on the other hand, is a similar practice, but with a more specific focus on connecting with the Earth and the energy of nature. It's a way of feeling rooted, safe and connected to the energy of the Earth.

To carry out rooting, follow these steps:

Start by finding a quiet, comfortable place to sit or stand.

Close your eyes and take a few deep breaths to relax your body and calm your mind.

Imagine that from the base of your spine or feet, deep roots are growing towards the Earth's core.

Feel these roots extending and intertwining with the Earth's energy, like the roots of a tree.

Visualize the nourishing and powerful energy of the Earth rising up through your roots and filling your whole body with a sense of security and stability.

Remain in this visualization maintaining a sense of rootedness for a few minutes, sitting connected and balanced with the Earth.

Rooting is a technique that connects you with the energy of nature, reminding you of your connection with the world around you. It's a powerful practice that keeps you centered and rooted in the midst of life's changes and challenges. By rooting yourself, you recognize that the Earth is the cradle of physical life, the only place where the physical and the spiritual manifest in a conscious way. Remember, your physical body belongs to the Earth and you will return to it.

In this rooting process, you establish a deep connection with the Earth, just like the roots of a tree that spread out and intertwine in the soil. This connection nourishes and strengthens your energy and provides a sense of security and stability on your spiritual journey.

By mentalizing your connection to the Earth, you recognize the importance of honoring and respecting nature, as it is the support of all physical life. This awareness reminds you of your responsibility to take care of your environment and all the life forms that inhabit it.

The regular practice of rooting brings a sense of inner peace, balance and connection with the present. When you feel rooted, you are better prepared to face life's challenges with clarity and confidence. By staying connected to your essence and purpose, you connect with that which gives you life.

36
Harmony of Nature with the Universe

Living in harmony with nature and the universe is a deep and meaningful quest for many spiritual seekers. Your connection with nature and the cosmos is intrinsic, and when you recognize and honor this connection, you experience a deep sense of belonging and balance.

One of the first steps to living in harmony with nature and the universe is to recognize the interconnectedness of everything. Understand that you are an integral part of the vast fabric of life, and that every living being and natural element plays an important role in this interdependent web. By adopting this awareness, you develop respect for all forms of life and for ecological balance.

Gratitude is a powerful spiritual practice that helps cultivate a sense of appreciation and connection. Take time every day to express gratitude for the beauty and bounty of nature around you. This can be done through a simple pause to admire the landscape, giving thanks for the food you eat or even writing a gratitude journal dedicated to nature. This practice of gratitude creates a deep bond with the natural world, reminding you of your responsibility to protect it.

Nature has profound wisdom and a series of cycles that govern the functioning of the universe. By observing and learning from these cycles you adjust your lifestyle to be in tune with natural harmony. Observe the seasons, the movement of the tides, the rising and setting of the sun, and how animals and plants adapt to these changes. By tuning in to these natural rhythms, you adjust your activities and spiritual practices to be more in line with the flow of the universe.

Living in harmony with nature also involves a conscious relationship with natural resources. When using resources such as water, energy and food, do so with awareness and moderation. Try to reduce excessive consumption, reuse and recycle whenever possible and opt for renewable energy sources. By taking these measures, you contribute to the preservation of natural resources and the balance of the planet.

The Earth is a living and sacred being, and it is important to honor this sacredness. Find ways to connect with the Earth in a reverent and respectful way. Spend time outdoors, walk barefoot in the grass, hug trees or hold gratitude ceremonies in natural spaces. These practices strengthen your connection with the Earth, it is the recognition of the divine presence in all creation

Take responsibility for being a guardian of nature, caring for the environment and defending the rights of living beings. Take part in conservation initiatives, support environmental organizations, be an example of sustainable practices. By acting as a guardian of nature, you are contributing to the preservation of the planet and to a more balanced and healthy future.

Living in harmony with nature and the universe is a journey of awareness, connection and respect. As you recognize this interconnectedness and adopt practices of gratitude, learning and conscious care, you align yourself with the flow of the universe, becoming an agent of positive change. May these practices inspire you to live in harmony with nature, honoring and preserving the beauty and wisdom of the natural world.

37
Relationships

Deep Connections

On the spiritual journey, relationships play a fundamental role in growth, learning and transformation. As you seek a deeper connection with your inner self and the divine, you also seek meaningful and authentic connections with others.

Relationships are like mirrors that reflect your journey of growth and self-knowledge. Each person who comes into your life brings with them valuable lessons and opportunities to learn. These encounters are full of meaning, as they teach you to practice love, compassion, patience and forgiveness, fundamental skills for spiritual development.

By relating to others, you are challenged and inspired to face aspects of yourself that you may ignore or avoid. These experiences help expand your consciousness, allowing you to better understand who you are and how you interact with the world around you.

Relationships are a constant source of growth and learning, as each person you connect with teaches you something new about yourself and life. Through interactions with others, you have the opportunity to confront your fears, challenge your limiting beliefs and overcome your weaknesses.

In addition, relationships offer support, encouragement and celebration as you move forward on your spiritual journey. You meet people who support you in your goals and encourage you to keep going, even in the most challenging times. These positive relationships help you feel more confident and determined in your quest for personal growth.

It's important to remember that relationships are not only about what you can receive, but also about what you can give. By practicing love and compassion in your relationships, you create a safe and welcoming space for others, allowing them to grow and develop too.

Therefore, by nurturing and valuing the relationships in your life, you recognize the transformative power they have on your spiritual journey. Each connection, whether short or long term, brings with it a wealth of experiences and learnings that help you become a more conscious, compassionate and loving human being.

Prioritize relationships that are nourishing, supporting your spiritual growth. Look for people who share similar interests such as values and worldviews. Seek connections with people who inspire, encourage and challenge you to expand your consciousness. This can include friends, partners, spiritual mentors or members of spiritual communities.

Cultivate empathy in your relationships, seeking to understand the perspectives of others, showing genuine compassion. Empathy is the ability to put yourself in the other person's shoes and understand their experiences and feelings. Unconditional love is another important aspect. Love others without judgment or expectations, recognizing the divine essence that resides in each one, allowing them to be who they are.

Sharing spiritual experiences with others strengthens connections and creates a sense of community and mutual support. Find ways to share your insights, spiritual practices and stories of transformation with like-minded people. This can be done through sincere conversations, participation in spiritual study groups, retreats or spiritual sharing events.

Challenges in relationships are opportunities for growth and healing. Sometimes conflicts, disagreements and challenging situations can arise in your relationships. See these moments as invitations to deepen your understanding, practice forgiveness, develop patience and seek loving solutions. Relational challenges can catalyze greater spiritual growth if approached with awareness and a willingness to learn.

Remember that the inner journey is the basis for healthy and meaningful relationships. The more deeply connected you are with yourself and your own spirituality, the more authentically you can relate to others. Dedicate time to self-care, spiritual practices, meditation and self-reflection. By nurturing your own spiritual growth, you will have more to offer the relationships you cultivate.

Building and maintaining deep and meaningful relationships is an essential part of the spiritual journey. As you connect with others in an authentic and loving way, you create a field of mutual support and growth. Cultivating nourishing relationships, practicing conscious communication and sharing spiritual experiences contributes to your own expansion and to the flourishing of everyone involved.

38
Service to Others

On the spiritual path, service to others plays a fundamental role. It is through love and generosity that you can express your connection with the divine, contributing to collective well-being.

Service to others is an expression of compassion and altruistic love. It is the conscious act of dedicating time, energy, skills and resources to benefit and help others. Service is not limited to grandiose actions, but can be expressed in simple gestures of kindness.

Each of us has unique gifts and abilities to offer. Discover your passions, interests and talents and find ways to use them in service to others. Ask yourself how you can use your skills to make a difference in people's lives.

Generosity is another essential aspect of service. Be generous with your time, attention, resources and love. Be willing to share what you have, whether material or emotional. Generosity is not just about giving tangible things, but also about offering compassion, understanding and emotional support.

An act of love and service is being present and listening with empathy when someone shares their experiences, challenges or joys. Take the time to be fully present, listen carefully and offer support. Sometimes all people need is someone to listen and understand.

A powerful way to serve others is through volunteering and participating in communities. Find organizations or groups that align with your passions and values and offer your time and skills. This could involve working in shelters, helping with food drives, participating in environmental conservation projects, among many others.

Don't underestimate the power of small acts of kindness. A smile, a kind word, a gesture of help or an attentive listen can make a significant difference to someone's life. Look for daily opportunities to practice small acts of love and generosity in your relationships, at work or in your community.

While service to others is essential, it's also important to remember to take care of yourself. Make time for self-care, to recharge your energy and nurture your own spiritual journey. By taking care of yourself, you will be better able to serve others in a meaningful and sustainable way.

By practicing service to others and performing acts of love and generosity, you expand your consciousness and connect with the deepest essence of cosmic spirituality. As you serve, you become a channel for divine love, strengthening the web of connection that unites all beings in something greater. Remember that service is not an obligation, but a privilege and an opportunity to grow and contribute to a better world.

Acknowledgements

As we come to the end of this book, I want to express my deep gratitude to you, the reader, who has dedicated yourself to exploring this content by embarking on a spiritual journey. It has been an honor to share this knowledge and reflection with you.

On this journey, we have discussed various topics related to Cosmic Spirituality, from healing and energy balance to conscious manifestation and the expansion of consciousness. I sincerely hope that the words in this book have touched your life in some way, inspiring and guiding you on your own spiritual path.

Remember, the spiritual quest is an individual and unique journey, and it is a privilege to be able to accompany you on part of your journey. Remember that you have immense power within you and that the connection with the divine is always accessible. Stay open, curious and committed to your personal and spiritual growth.

I would also like to express my gratitude to the Beings of Light who inspire and guide us. Cosmic energy and other forms of wisdom give us a deeper understanding of ourselves, the universe and our connection to all that is.

I would also like to thank those who contributed directly to the creation of this book, from the researchers and scholars who shared their knowledge to the editors, designers and editorial team who helped shape these words.

Finally, I would like to express my gratitude to you, the reader, for dedicating your time and energy to this book. I hope that the information and practices shared have been valuable to you on your spiritual journey. May they continue to inspire and enlighten your path, allowing you to connect with your divine essence and manifest your true cosmic nature.

If you have felt the call to delve even deeper into Cosmic Spirituality, remember that this is only part of the vast knowledge available. Keep exploring, studying and practicing. Let your intuition be your guide and follow the path that resonates with your heart.

May this book have planted seeds of transformation and awakening in your life. May it have helped expand your consciousness, bringing clarity and understanding. And may you move forward, inspired and empowered, creating a reality aligned with your most authentic essence.

With love, light and gratitude.